MARK STEVENS

The Last Club Kid

Money Success Fame Glamour

First published by Mark Stevens Publishing 2026

First edition

Illustration by Casual Clyde
Editing by Dave Watkins

This book was professionally typeset on Reedsy.
Find out more at reedsy.com

Contents

The Last Club Kid

Mark Stevens

For Paloma Picasso—A diva before her time

Her light, her laughter, her legend.
   You taught me that sequins could be armor
   and that every night deserved its own kind of grace.

And for all the performers, talents, and entertainers
   of South Beach, New York, and Houston
   who lit up the night during this era—
   especially those who are no longer with us.

The dance floor remembers. And so do I.

Foreword

by Superstar DJ Keoki

I've played records all over the world, but South Beach in the '90s was different. That wasn't just nightlife—that was belief. That's where the night became a religion, and everyone inside was a true believer.

The first time I met Ghost, he was just a kid out of Houston—platform shoes, smeared face paint, looking like he'd gotten dressed in the dark with nothing but nerve. He didn't belong there. No connections. No money. No lineage.

But he had it.

You can't teach someone how to understand the night. You either feel it in your bones, or you don't. Everyone else is just a tourist in sequins. Ghost felt it. He didn't perform at the room—he merged with it. Authentic. Fearless. All in. Every moment.

The club kid scene was never just about parties. It was about alchemy—taking everything broken, ugly, and cruel in the world and turning it into something beautiful, if only until the sun came up. Ghost understood that. He lived it. And like anyone who goes too deep, too fast, too far, he paid the price.

This book tells the truth in ways most nightlife memoirs won't. Mark doesn't polish the madness or pretend the crash didn't hurt. He tells you what it gave him.

What it took.

What it cost.

If you've ever wondered what it was really like—past the velvet ropes, beyond the mythology, underneath the glitter—this is the story.

Ghost is gone.

Mark survived.

And this is a story worth hearing.

Acknowledgments

For my friends and family, who stood by me through my crazy days and addictions—especially my oldest sister, Sam, who is no longer with us but was with me through many of these adventures. Kelly, her daughter, who is like my own child and has seen me through so many trying times. My extended nieces and nephews, my brothers and sisters, procreated in my absence. Special mention to those who helped with my sister's arrangements when she passed--you know who you are.

To Superstar DJ Keoki, thank you for years of memories both in person and over the airwaves—and for honoring this book with your foreword. To Mikey (DJ NutZ) for rescuing me in the stories in this book, and many times not mentioned. To Chris Alan for believing in me and always having my back. To David (DJ Fusion) and Elisabeth Piccone for believing in me when no one else did. To Bennie and Brandy for being lifelong friends and putting up with my drama for several decades. To the Vox family, Keeley and Art, for looking out for Sammijo and helping guide me through the current nightlife vibe in order to promote the book.

A great big thank you to the Beta readers and their feedback, which helped me realize some pacing issues; to my cover artist, Casual Clyde, for bringing my vision to life; and to my copyeditor, Dave, for guiding the rough draft into a final, readable version.

Please Note

Some names, including the author's, have been changed for anonymity and to protect the innocent.

There are no photographs included in this memoir. The club kid scene that I was inducted into in Houston operated under a strict code: "Remain anonymous." In an era before smartphones and social media, what happened in the clubs stayed in the clubs. The few images that existed from that time have been lost to the years, moves, and the chaos that followed. What remains are the memories—vivid, visceral, and as close to the truth as memory allows.

This story is told from the author's recollection of events that occurred between 1993 and 2005. Conversations have been reconstructed from memory and are not verbatim. Some timelines have been compressed for narrative flow. The emotional truth of these experiences remains intact.

Introduction

My name is Mark Stevens, but soon you'll know me as Ghost. I'm in my fifties now, writing this from a quiet apartment in Houston—far from the chaos that once defined me. But in 1989, I was sixteen, closeted, and desperate for a world where I could finally breathe.

Growing up with an abusive, alcoholic father, I made myself a promise early on: I would never drink. I didn't whisper it or say it dramatically. It lived inside me quietly, the way children make private vows to protect themselves when adults fail to do so. I watched alcohol turn my father into someone unpredictable, volatile, and dangerous. I saw the way fear could fill a house more quickly than smoke. Those memories left scars—emotional, physical, and invisible—and they shaped my idea of what addiction meant. To me, addiction looked like a bottle, a fist, a slurred voice, a slammed door.

So I stayed away from alcohol with a kind of rigid moral discipline. If alcohol turned him into a monster, then avoiding it would keep me safe. That was my logic. That was my shield.

But trauma doesn't simply disappear because you refuse one substance. And vows made in childhood don't prepare you for the temptations that arrive in adulthood dressed as something else—something that doesn't look like the thing that hurt you.

By avoiding alcohol so fiercely, I left a door open without realizing it. Not because I wanted drugs. Not because I was looking for an escape. But because I thought I knew what addiction looked like—and drugs weren't part of that picture. Alcohol was the enemy. Everything else seemed foreign, distant, harmless in comparison.

And so, the first time I used drugs, it wasn't some dramatic moment of rebellion. It wasn't even a fully made choice. I was given ecstasy one night—offered it with the same casual tone someone might offer a drink, and innocently took it. The next night, it was LSD. I didn't know that those two nights were about to redraw the map of my life. All I knew then was that, for the first time, something lit up inside me. Something clicked. Something came alive that I would spend many years chasing.

I didn't recognize that this was the beginning. That the same vow which had kept me from alcohol had also blinded me to other risks. That trauma had left openings I didn't understand. That addiction doesn't always enter through the front door. Sometimes it slips in through the only space you never thought to guard.

That weekend didn't just introduce me to drugs.

It introduced me to the version of myself who would seek them out for years to come.

* * *

It started at a club called Heaven.

Six giant video screens looping MTV-style videos from that period. Fog rolling across the floor, tinted pink and blue. The smell of smoke and cologne. The bass so deep that it rearranges your organs.

And TJ——the doorman with a white-painted face and jeweled eyelids, platform sneakers making him impossibly tall. He looked like he'd stepped out of a dream. People whispered secrets to him and disappeared into the crowd.

I was sixteen with a fake ID, walking into a world I didn't know existed.

That night was my first glimpse of the club kid world—a living art movement that transformed nightlife into a theatrical experience.

I didn't know it yet, but Heaven was my initiation.

A decade later, I'd become one of them.

A decade later, I'd become Ghost.

* * *

Years after, long after the noise and color of those nights had started to fade into memory, I found myself on an entirely different path—one I never would have predicted back when I was sixteen and chasing bass lines through the city. I went back to school, got an education, and eventually became an addiction counselor and later a college professor.

In recovery, there's a phrase you hear often: *people, places, and things.* You change them to stay sober—to break the patterns that once consumed you.

But back then, in those early days of my nightlife education, *people, places, and things* meant something different. They were the building blocks of who I was becoming. Each person taught me something about the world. Each place stamped itself into my DNA. Each thing—a beat, a light, a whispered invitation—pulled me a little further into the life that would shape me.

In my fifties, I can admit that some details have blurred. Names fade. Faces soften. Memories shift like fog caught in a warehouse strobe. I've checked with friends, cross-referenced stories, and pieced together timelines as best I can. What I'm writing here is as accurate as memory allows—the essence of what happened, the feeling of it, the reality of the world we lived in.

And part of that truth is this: We were Generation X. We helped build the early days of rave culture. We survived the chaos of a world no one warned us about.

I want to honor the people who stood beside me in the peaks and valleys— even if a name or a detail isn't perfect. I want to capture the pulse of those nights, the raw hunger for belonging, the way music could glue entire strangers together into a single heartbeat.

I

Awakening

Houston, early 1990s. A kid who didn't fit anywhere discovered a world where not fitting in was the whole point. Under strobes and bass, surrounded by drag queens and ravers, platform shoes and PLUR bracelets, Ghost was born—not as an escape, but as the truest version of a self that had been hiding for years. This is the story of finding your tribe in the dark, learning to dance before you can walk, and realizing that sometimes the people who seem the most lost are actually leading the way.

1

Heaven

Looking back to the 1980s, my dad was something of a gangster—fortunate for me, depending on how you look at it.

He was the kind of man who could make a call and get things done, no questions asked. A television repairman who learned the trade during one of his many stints in prison, he had a way with people and spent his days crisscrossing Houston, picking up TVs—huge ones in big wooden boxes—to haul back to Channelview on the east side, where I grew up.

My parents ran a TV and radio repair shop built out in the front of the double-wide trailer where we lived, just off Interstate 10. Our family had lived in that part of Harris County for generations. My great-grandmother, who helped raise me, had worked as a munitions director at the old ordnance depot— hundreds of bunkers filled with World War II ammunition. I grew up in the shadow of the San Jacinto Monument, the birthplace of Texas independence, just across the shipping lane from Channelview.

The best way to describe myself as a kid is "special." People didn't really use the word autistic then, but I did things no one my age did. At ten, dissatisfied with our tiny branch library, I wrote a letter to the commissioners' court demanding a new one. They actually brought me in, listened to me, and promised to build it. (The North Channel Branch on Wallisville Road opened in 1998.)

By twelve, my mom and my grandmother—a seamstress—had sewn me a clown costume, I was called Do Nut, and I spent weekends doing grand openings and birthday parties to save for my driver's license and my first car.

But the most crucial turning point came at thirteen. One Saturday morning, I saw a local kids' show calling for child reporters. I mailed in a story idea, and a few months later, after a short ferry ride across the channel to the Monument, I filmed my segment. It aired that spring, and the producer invited me to be a VIP guest at the Texas Sesquicentennial celebration at the Monument the following year. At fifteen, I was hanging around the shopping center a few blocks behind my parents' TV shop. I had done some odd jobs for the owner of the local liquor store, who also owned the shopping center.

Around this time, I began asking about a space in his shopping center that had been vacant for several years. That became my first (short-lived) restaurant, Hot Dogs Etc. The place where I would play "Only in My Dreams" by Debbie Gibson on the jukebox at closing each night. It was the place and time where I first learned that I was a dreamer.

I wasn't questioning my sexuality yet, but I soon would be with the arrival of Gary Y. He arrived in Channelview the year I was a freshman, slipping into our small high-school ecosystem like a spark landing in dry grass. We were the same age, both in choir, both trying to figure out the shape of ourselves, but Gary had something I didn't: he was out. Openly. Unapologetic. In the late 1980s in Texas, to be queer or even hint at being gay was taboo. People whispered. Teachers blinked too hard. But Gary walked down the halls like he was immune to gravity.

I noticed him the first day when he sang, with that effortless confidence, that softness, that edge.

And I was done for.

We became friends in the strange, tentative way two queer kids find each other before they have the language to understand why they're drawn together. Sometimes after school, I'd go hang out at his house, sitting cross-legged on his bedroom floor while he mesmerized me with stories from the boarding school he'd attended before moving to town. Stories about boys kissing boys in dorm rooms, about experimenting behind locked doors, about things that were thrilling and terrifying and felt like someone describing a planet I wasn't brave enough to visit yet.

I didn't know what to do with the attraction. I didn't even have the vocabulary for it. But I knew it was real.

Gary had a way of leaning back on his bed, hands behind his head, recounting those stories as if they were gospel. My stomach would twist—not with jealousy, but possibility. Something in me was waking up.

At the choir showcase that year, he performed George Michael's "Careless Whisper." And God—he didn't just sing it. He lived it. Every note was drenched in a kind of longing I recognized before I understood it. His voice wrapped around that song like he was confessing something, and the room felt electric, charged with queerness.

Nobody said it aloud, but everyone felt it.

Gary made friends with my neighbors down the street, Smiley and Beau— the kind of guys who knew every detail about Madonna's tours and could reconstruct her stage sets out of conversation alone. When Madonna launched her 1990 Blonde Ambition tour and filmed in Houston, their house turned into a Harlem ballroom. We gathered around the TV like it was church, all of us teenagers with too-big feelings and nowhere to put them. Not long after, we watched the video for "Vogue," attempting our best hand movements for a makeshift voguing competition.

Gary Y was the first door that cracked open in me. Not the door to nightlife— the door to *truth*. To queerness. To the possibility. Gary didn't push me through it. He just let the light in.

I still needed someone to teach me how to step through. That someone was waiting for me, as I would discover not long after, in a club called Heaven.

* * *

By sixteen, all I wanted was to work at AstroWorld, Houston's legendary amusement park. You had to be eighteen, but my dad sorted that out. He made a few calls and handed me a freshly laminated fake ID. That ID didn't just get me a job—it drew back the veil to a world I didn't know existed.

Houston back then was a strange kind of city—hot asphalt by day, a mystery by night. Montrose was its heartbeat, an oasis for the misfits, the dreamers, the ones figuring themselves out. The streets smelled of fried food and cigarette smoke. Neon signs hummed like lullabies. You could drive ten minutes in any direction and find something you weren't supposed to.

When I got my first car—a beat-up Chevy Citation that smelled like old French fries—freedom tasted like possibility. My high-school friends wanted Galveston. There was no way for me to know at the time, but this trip would be my first exposure to the party and drug-taking underworld. Besides, I wanted anywhere that wasn't church, wasn't my bedroom, wasn't the closet I was still locked inside.

We took Beltway 8 down to 45 South, windows down, music blasting—probably C+C Music Factory, The KLF, or Deee-Lite, the soundtrack of my secret life. When we crossed the causeway, the Houston skyline shrinking behind us, I felt something loosen in my chest.

Stewart Beach Club was nothing like what I would experience months later at Heaven. It was straight, touristy, filled with families and sunburned tourists. But for a few hours, I danced in the daylight—something I never did, something that felt dangerous and thrilling. My friends, especially my closest and unfortunate straight crush at the time, Devon, didn't know I was memorizing the moves, studying the freedom, planning my escape.

Afterward, at Whataburger, Devon approached a beautiful young woman at a nearby table.

"Are those tabs?" he asked, pointing at a small pile of colorful pills that she was trying to conceal with her palm on her table.

She looked at us—sixteen, sunburned, obviously too young—and smiled. "Not for you, sweetie."

I stayed quiet, tasting salt on my lips, already dreaming of the clubs I'd read about in magazines—the places where gay boys like me could finally be noticed. On the ride home to Channelview, I asked Devon why he was so interested in tabs.

"Simple," Devon said. "They make you feel good and leave the cares of this world behind. You experience sounds and touch supernaturally ... oh, and your eyes roll in the back of your head."

My relationship with Devon was one of my earliest memories of having a crush on a straight guy. One tune in particular on the radio on the ride home was prophetic: "Enjoy the Silence" by Depeche Mode. I tried to do just that. I remember us becoming close, as he was emo way before it was a thing. However, when I called his house one night, his mother answered and questioned why I was being so friendly with her son. For me, it was more about attraction and confusion with how the world worked—one of many disappointments I would face due to my attractions over the years.

* * *

Within months of that first trip and with the confidence to drive anywhere, my friend Cheryl was the first to say, "You have to see this club. It's called Heaven." She was still figuring herself out, too. We both were. I didn't use words like *gay* or *queer* yet—those felt too big, too dangerous. But curiosity was enough.

It was a humid Friday when we went. The asphalt steamed under yellow streetlights as we drove my Chevy downtown, the fake ID in my wallet a secret against my hip. Heaven sat on a residential corner in Montrose—just a dark, industrial-looking brick building from the outside.

The bass hit before I even saw the dance floor—thick, physical, vibrating through my ribs like I'd stepped too close to a passing train. Cheryl gripped my arm as the doorman lifted the velvet rope and waved us inside. As the doorman put the rope back in place, the world outside dissolved, as if it had never existed at all.

Inside Heaven, there was no past or future—only rhythm.

Lisa Stansfield glowed from the massive video screens overhead—— "Been around the world and I, I, I ..." and I swear she was singing directly to me. I didn't recognize a single face in the club, but it didn't matter. Everyone there was fully alive, moving as though they had finally found the only place they fit.

Light cut through the fog in sharp, colored beams. Sequins and sweat glittered like stars. Cigarette smoke curled upward and dissolved into the strobes, maybe lust, maybe the exact mixture of both that defined the late-night world I was stepping into.

Cheryl came in close and screamed, "This place is insane!"

"I think I love it!" I yelled back.

And I did.

We danced until we were gasping for breath, our sweat mixing with the fog that hugged the floor. The crowd moved like a single body—a living organism stitched together by bass, laughter, and the electricity of strangers who felt like immediate family. Every strobe was a pulse. Every cheer felt like a prayer.

At one point, I found myself alone at the bar, catching my breath. That's when he appeared—the doorman who had captivated me on the way in. TJ drifted through the haze like a spirit made of glitter and bone. People orbited him instinctively, leaning in to whisper secrets I wasn't yet allowed to hear.

There was something mythological about him even in the way he stood— still, poised, powerful. He wasn't trying to be anyone. He *was*, and the room rearranged itself around that fact.

Nearby, another club kid strutted by with ponytails made of stacked colorful rings—like a toddler's toy re-imagined as couture. Everywhere I turned, something surreal shimmered past.

A sweet, muscular guy approached me with his partner—a short, soft-spoken Latino man—two of the kindest people I'd ever met. We danced, we laughed, we shouted introductions over the music. Years later, during White Party in South Beach, the muscular one spotted me across the room and said, "You were that kid from Heaven, right?" And I was. I always would be.

But hovering over the entire scene now, with hindsight, was a shadow—one I couldn't see then. I was sixteen in 1989, and only a few years later, almost all the men in that room, an entire generation of gay men aged twenty to fifty, would vanish to HIV and AIDS. So many lost their lives that the brightness of the night was extinguished for an entire generation of young gay men. Back then, we didn't know the cliff we were dancing beside.

But that night, none of it mattered. I was a teenager with a fake ID, a head full of rhythm, and the unshakable feeling that I'd wandered into the beginning of the rest of my life.

Hours later, when the sun finally dragged itself over the skyline, Cheryl and I sat on the curb outside Heaven, laughing at nothing. The air smelled like dew. Sweat clung to my shirt. My ears rang with phantom bass. Heaven was still inside me, vibrating like a secret heartbeat.

"You're never going to be the same, are you?" she asked.

"No," I said. "I don't think I am."

And she was right. The night had chosen me. It whispered through the fog and sequins and sweat: *You're one of us now.*

And from that moment forward—I was.

That night changed everything. But I couldn't have done it alone.

* * *

Cheryl and I were inseparable during those days. She lived across the street from my uncle. Her hair was usually short and dyed some wild color—pink, blue, whatever matched her mood. She carried a spark in her that lit her from within. She was fearless in ways I wasn't yet. If someone asked about her sexuality, she'd shrug and say, "I'm a girl who likes girls," with the kind of ease I envied. I was still unraveling my own truths quietly, gently, cautiously.

Week after week, Cheryl grabbed my hand and shouted, "Promise me we're coming back next Friday!" And we did. Heaven became our ritual. Our refuge. Our religion. Friday nights were countdowns. Saturday mornings were revelations. Within minutes of stepping inside, the world outside lost all power over us.

That's when I learned the first rule of nightlife: The night can love you. But it can try to own you, too.

When Cheryl's parents eventually placed her in treatment for emotional and addiction issues, I felt the loneliness hit like a cold wind. But I had already memorized the route downtown, already learned the rhythm of the neon; I already belonged to the night.

And the night--the clubs, the drama, the after-hours--wasn't done with me yet. But I took a break from nightclubs to explore the other offerings of the gay area known as Montrose.

* * *

After a few timid steps through Montrose and a handful of anonymous brushes with a community I was still learning how to enter, I found myself volunteering on the Gay and Lesbian Switchboard, and also at KPFT, the Pacifica radio station, for a Friday night queer-focused program hosted by two couples: each a gay man married to a lesbian, each in their own nonlinear constellation of queer love. They fascinated me. Their lives were messy and honest and decades ahead of their time.

One night, during a show, the phone rang.

The voice on the other end was soft, nervous, and somehow familiar. It was Geary B—a boy I'd known in passing, but hearing him on the line that night made something in my chest shift.

We talked.

We connected.

We kept talking.

And then we met.

He was younger than me—still figuring out his place in the world the way I was figuring out mine—but the connection felt immediate, bright, intoxicating in a way I had no defenses against. Within weeks, we were inseparable. Within months, we were living together.

It wasn't dramatic or dangerous.

It wasn't some forbidden, shadowy romance.

It was soft.

Awkward.

Tender.

Bright in the way only first love can be.

We tried to build a life inside that little bubble—working odd jobs, taking calls, spinning records at KPFT, navigating a world that was changing faster than we could keep up with. We were young. Too young, honestly. Eventually, the cracks showed. We grew in different directions. And when I left for Bible college in Waxahachie, we let each other go in the kindest way two kids can.

But he was my first boyfriend.

My first mirror.

My first "us."

Geary wasn't the spark.

He was the flame.

2

Ghost Story

By seventeen, I experienced the first of many temporary detours in my life.

I tried to escape to Bible college in Waxahachie, Texas, just south of Dallas—not once, but twice. Each time, I boarded a plane and flew away from everything I had ever known, convinced that maybe this time I could pray myself into alignment. Perhaps this time, I could become the person everyone expected me to be.

I wanted to do the right thing, or at least what I understood "right" to mean. I wanted to inspire, to guide, to fit into the world of waking up for 7 a.m. classes and researching Bible verses. Training to become a children's minister felt like the path I was supposed to take. But somewhere deep inside, something didn't match.

I couldn't reconcile who I was with marrying a woman and having children. I didn't have the language yet—didn't have the courage yet—to admit the truth to myself. Instead, I buried it under scripture and chapel hours and the desperate hope that maybe I could transform myself through sheer force of will.

I did find some success running the on-campus cafe. I was in my element there—decorating it like an actual lion's den, playing Christian techno, creating something that felt like mine. For spring, summer, and fall, I convinced myself it was enough.

Then one night during my second attempt, I snuck away from campus and saw Madonna's *Truth or Dare* which had just opened in theaters. It cracked something open. On screen, she was raw, unfiltered, honest to the bone. She confessed desire, claimed her identity, and flaunted her imperfections. She didn't apologize for existing. Watching her felt like watching someone say aloud everything I was too afraid to whisper.

By the time the credits rolled, I knew I couldn't keep lying—not to God, not to anyone, and especially not to myself.

Shortly after, the Bible College asked me to leave. They couched it in polite terms, but the truth was simple: I no longer fit there. Both times, my overall grade-point average had dropped below 2.0, and I found myself on academic probation. Both times, the dean of academics sent me home.

Bible college was a diversion I had to take to learn that I couldn't run from who I was. But leaving that cage didn't mean I was ready to go home to Houston.

I found a room north of Waxahachie in the Oaklawn neighborhood of Dallas, and the city opened up to me slowly at first, as though it was testing me whether I deserved its secrets. I wandered through Oak Lawn and Cedar Springs, drawn by the neon glow, the hum of music behind thick doors, and the promise that somewhere in that maze, people were living the way I could only imagine.

And just like that, Dallas became my classroom.

The first major landmark on that map was The Village Station ... a legendary gay club on Cedar Springs that later became known as Station 4. Walking through its doors felt like entering another universe--one with its own planets, each with its own gravity.

The crowd was older, sleeker, sharper. The crowd in Oak Lawn moved with a confidence I didn't yet understand—a different kind of wildness than Houston's scene. It wasn't about rebellion; it was about ownership. These were men and women who had decided who they were long before I dared even to ask myself the question.

It was there that I first encountered the Dallas club kids. They were a world unto themselves—platform boots, vinyl jackets, glittered skin, and T-shirts that screamed *Generation X* like a declaration. They were sophisticated and strange at the same time, like they'd stepped out of a music video and landed in the heart of Texas.

One of them, Lawrence, eyed me with a mix of amusement and curiosity.

"You're not really a club kid," he said, leaning in with a smirk. "You're like a country kid pretending."

He wasn't wrong. I was still figuring out my edges, testing identities like costumes, trying to see which one made me feel the most like myself. His comment didn't insult me—it made me laugh. I was pretending, and maybe pretending was the first step toward becoming.

Upstairs, the Rose Room buzzed with anticipation for its nightly ritual: The dating game run by host and comedian Paul J. Williams. Somehow, I got dragged into the lineup—me, a Garth Brooks lookalike contestant with boots and a cowboy hat. When I stepped onstage and tipped my hat with a "Howdy, boys!" the crowd erupted. It was ridiculous, but the laughter felt like oxygen.

It was the first moment I realized I could perform—not as a character, but as myself.

That same night, I saw Elaine Lancaster for the first time. She moved like royalty, every gesture deliberate, every inch of her dripping with poise. She wasn't just doing drag—she *was* drag, the living embodiment of confidence. Our paths would cross again years later in South Beach, but even that first sighting marked something in me.

If drag queens were superheroes, she was one of the ones who already knew what their power was and how to use it.

* * *

For a brief moment, I wondered if drag might be my destiny.

I tried it just once—a single night, a single transformation. My drag name? Samantha Cox. One of the local Latina queens painted my face with the kind of precision that felt like a blessing. A friend loaned me a wig. I squeezed into a dress that felt more like armor than fabric.

We walked the streets of Oak Lawn together in a tiny procession, and I entered the nightly talent contest at Big Daddy's, a bar with a stage and nightly talent contests featuring drag performers, singers, and such. I performed Taylor Dayne's "I'll Be Your Shelter"—dramatically, emotionally, maybe even a little off-key.

But the applause felt good.

I didn't win, of course. An older Black woman with a cane and a voice made of gold belted "Chain of Fools" and brought the house down. She deserved every second of victory.

Afterward, walking from Big Daddy's toward The Village Station, I ran into the entertainment director from the Rose Room. He stared at me—at Samantha—and said, "I recognized your eyes."

A thrilling punch to the gut.

Recognition, even in transformation. The diva and entertainment director from the Rose Room knew who I was from my appearances at the Rose Room dating game that he had hosted.

Years later in South Beach, I'd think back to that moment—how queens out of drag often passed unrecognized, like superheroes stripped of their masks. But Samantha didn't feel like my path. What called to me wasn't femininity. It was a transformation itself—the idea of becoming larger than life *without ceasing to be me.*

Drag is an art form.

But I needed something different.

Something closer to the bone.

Samantha Cox retired that night.

Ghost, however, had begun to stir.

Legends aren't born. They're assembled—piece by piece, foam and glitter, one late night at a time.

* * *

In Dallas, I'd gone through a carousel of roommates—most of them people I met at the Round-Up Saloon, where, on Sunday nights, the men and women who desperately wanted to learn to dance converged for Country and Western lessons. I became a regular, two-stepping and line dancing like it was a second language, thanks to Juanita, the instructor who could lead a herd of cattle if she needed to. That's where I met Michelle, my dance partner, and Bobby, who eventually became one of my closest friends.

Bobby and I moved into a small house off Central Expressway with a rotating cast of honorary roommates—Mario among them, who introduced us to Selena's music. I remember the first time I heard "Carcacha"—the rhythm, the joy, the way she made every note feel like a celebration. Those songs stitched themselves into my story.

Bobby's family embraced me instantly—his mother a social worker, his stepfather a high school counselor, both of them warm, open, and accepting in ways I wasn't used to. His stepfather had even written a book, *Awaken to Good Mourning*, a gentle guide to navigating grief. The title alone stuck with me.

Being around them taught me something about family—the chosen kind, the kind that doesn't demand masks or conditions. The kind that sees you.

It was the first hint that the life waiting for me didn't have to look like the one I knew growing up in East Houston.

* * *

I had to eat, so I worked at food—Burger King, then Wendy's, bouncing between franchises as systems collapsed and managers fled. Eventually, I landed in Denton, managing a 24-hour Burger King across from the University of North Texas, feeding drunk college kids at 3 a.m. while planning my escape back to the dance floor. The job paid for platform shoes and party supplies. That's all it needed to do.

That's where I met Andrew and Frank—two regulars with hearts full of mischief and pockets empty of money. They were deep into the Dallas underground rave scene and insisted I join them.

"You'll fit right in," Andrew said.

"You're weird enough already."

He meant it as a compliment. I took it as a prophecy.

Once, after hiring Andrew, my district manager visited and frowned.

"Your store looks more like Lemon Avenue," he said—a reference to Oak Lawn and Cedar Springs—"than a college Burger King."

He meant it as a warning. I took it as pride.

It was early 1995 when everything sharpened into focus. I had just fallen in love with *Star Trek: Voyager*. Captain Janeway—poised, fearless, commanding chaos with a steady voice—became my unlikely role model. I wanted her confidence, her calm. I tried to navigate my life with that same kind of authority, even if I had no idea where my starship, also lost, would find itself.

Around the same time, Jack in the Box reemerged after an extended closure, plastering its comeback slogan everywhere: "Jack's Back." It felt like a sign, even if I didn't fully understand what it meant yet.

One freezing Friday night, Andrew and Frank convinced me to come to a rave in Deep Elm—the warehouse district of Dallas, where the nights always felt slightly dangerous and entirely alive. Amy, Frank's childhood friend and the daughter of the man who owned The Gas Pipe—the biggest headshop in Texas—joined us with her boyfriend, Brandon, and a pack of about ten others.

The line snaked around the building, and everyone was wearing their winter's finest—Inuit-looking jackets with fur and as much bundling as possible against the cold. Neon bracelets flickered. Breath turned into steam. The bass from inside thumped through the concrete like a living thing trying to escape.

Someone handed me a little white pill—MDMA—and without hesitation, I swallowed it.

When it hit, it was like the world exhaled and took me with it. Warmth spread from my chest to my fingertips, and suddenly I couldn't stop laughing.

Everything shimmered—the streetlights, the jackets, the icy air.

"Jack's back!" I shouted at total strangers, followed immediately by, "Beam me up, Janeway!"

The whole line erupted into laughter. It felt like the universe was laughing with us.

At the entrance stood a petite girl, flanked by two massive bouncers and a metal drum full of cash. She was the gatekeeper. I watched her scan groups like a psychic sorting souls.

Preppy boys? "A hundred each." They paid without blinking.

Ravers in neon? "Twenty apiece." A bargain.

Cowboy types? "This isn't your party. Move along." And they did.

When our group approached, she smirked. "You're with Amy?" She waved us all in for fifty bucks total.

Being connected to The Gas Pipe had its perks.

Inside, it felt like a portal had swallowed us whole. The warehouse was alive—walls dripping with condensation, fog machines on full blast, lights slicing the air. Two enormous screens dropped from the ceiling, playing psychedelic visuals that melted into lasers and strobes.

Our group had one rule: stay together.

Amy took it seriously, elbowing through the crowd, her eyes sharp. But something in the room kept pulling me away—not out of defiance, but instinct. I drifted through the music like a ghost moving between worlds. Yet every time Amy turned around, somehow I was right there beside her again.

Finally, she stopped, hands on her hips, laughing through confusion.

"Where do you keep disappearing to?" she asked. "It's like you're a ghost!"

The word hit me like destiny tapping my shoulder.

"Ghost."

It didn't feel like a nickname—it felt like the truth. Like something that had always been waiting for me to hear it.

A few hours later, a different kind of light appeared as flashlights from uniformed police officers pierced the room; the music stopped. The rave, once a living, breathing entity of fun, had been raided by law enforcement. Sirens pierced the music. Lights exploded against the fog. People screamed, scattering into the freezing night. Someone yelled, "Go to Smokestacks!"—the unofficial after-party location.

When we reached the car, I found a broken window and my CD player was missing. Snow blew in. I couldn't drive—my eyes were still rolling, my brain humming like an electric wire. Andrew and Frank took over as I sat shivering, replaying the moment Amy named me.

We did try Smokestacks—waited in the cold, stamping and clapping our hands together to keep the circulation going—but no one appeared. Eventually, we headed back to Denton.

But something had changed.

A joke had become an origin.

A broken window had cracked open a new identity.

A name had found its owner.

Every superhero has that moment—Bruce Wayne and the bat, Peter Parker and the spider.

Mine was a warehouse, a pill, a laugh, and a name whispered over bass.

That night, I wasn't just in the scene.

That night, I became Ghost.

* * *

The very next evening, we went to a club called SOA—short for "Sheets of acid." It was one of those places that only truly existed after midnight. The lights were low and hazy, the crowd moving like liquid mercury, the floor vibrating with possibility.

I sat cross-legged on the carpet in a corner, staring at a lava lamp like it was a constellation. Colors oozed and stretched in time with Basia's "New Day for You," melting perfectly into The Prodigy's "Broken Glass."

The carpet under me began to ripple. Not literally—but in my mind, it moved like water. I felt weightless. I felt unmade—in the best way.

Andrew and Frank laughed across the room, their voices echoing like they were underwater. And suddenly, for no reason at all, I started crying.

Not out of sadness.

Out of release.

Out of recognition.

Out of becoming.

Ghost wasn't a costume yet. TJ and the other club kids weren't just makeup and glitter. Ghost was a feeling—that suspended moment between who I had been and who I was about to become.

Every origin story starts with a transformation.

Mine began on that carpet.

We spent more weekends with Amy and Brandon at their apartment—lounging on beanbags, doing anything available to keep the party going and soften the comedown from the pills, watching MTV.

One of our final Dallas raves was at the Dallas Music Complex—a cavernous space filled with fog, strobes, and every kind of soul you could imagine.

A raver girl brought her gay best friend, and he and I spent half the night holding hands and making out in the open, dancing like the world didn't exist. At one point, a girl in the crowd started riding her boyfriend in plain view of everyone. Watching for fliers for upcoming parties, jumping into cars filled with ravers--this was the Dallas scene. It was also the night I first heard what would become one of my all-time favorite tracks: "The Bomb! (These Sounds Fall into My Mind)" by The Bucketheads.

Roxy and I would blast it in Houston months later—a song that felt like electricity in my veins. It became one of the soundtracks of my life—a song that never stopped moving.

* * *

Dallas was exhilarating, but it carried its own darkness.

Nights got longer.

Pills got heavier.

Reality thinned.

Most weekends, I stayed at Amy and Brandon's apartment. We'd find whatever party was happening, gather party supplies, and then collapse back at their place on Sunday mornings, watching *The Real World: San Francisco* while the world slowly came back into focus.

One Sunday, Amy and Brandon left to visit her parents. I stayed behind. That's when my body finally said no.

I started vomiting—violently, endlessly, my insides trying to expel something they couldn't name. Hours passed. The pain sharpened from nausea into something tighter, hotter, more insistent. By the time I realized something was seriously wrong, I could barely stand.

I don't remember the drive to Denton or walking into the ER. I remember white light, then nothing.

When I finally woke, my mother was sitting beside the hospital bed, her face pale and tight with the kind of fear that comes after relief. She told me my appendix had burst. The toxins had flooded my system. The doctors said I'd been close—too close.

They'd operated. I'd made it through. But I'd need weeks to heal.

She didn't ask about the pills, the parties, the life I'd been living in Dallas. She didn't need to. The silence between us said everything.

They drove me home to Houston without a word. Snow outside. Silence inside. My body was vibrating with the Ghost of nights that had almost killed me.

It was my first rescue.

My first reboot.

My first death, in a way.

Because every legend has a moment they almost don't survive.

And that was mine.

A year passed after Dallas tried to swallow me whole. I tried to be normal—whatever "normal" meant. I worked, slept, pretended. I tried daylight again. It never fit. The night echoed inside me like a distant bass line I could still feel through the floorboards of my life.

3

Becoming Ghost

After almost dying in Dallas, I found myself back in Montrose, ready to dive deeper. The nights started stretching beyond Heaven. After Cheryl left for emotional counseling and group therapy, I found Lori, a childhood church friend who now lived in the same complicated in-between space I did. She went by Roxy now, embracing a version of herself the church never knew what to do with. Her boyfriend, Keith, completed the trio. On weekends, we piled into a car and chased the hum of underground raves like moths around a streetlamp' to avoid partial rep of 'chased/chasing.'

The city had a pulse I hadn't learned to listen for yet—whispers passed between club kids, secret addresses scribbled on scraps of paper, fliers traded like relics. Heaven was the doorway, but behind it was a labyrinth.

Someone mentioned a place at 709 Franklin downtown. At the time, it was called Powertools—a raw, concrete warehouse filled with smoke, shadows, and electricity. Years later, the exact address would become Rehab, the club that would reshape after-hours in a few years.

The first time I walked into Powertools, it felt like stepping into the illicit boardroom of the city itself. Nothing was polished. Nothing was soft. The music was darker, faster, heavier—not the glossy, theatrical beats of Heaven, but something primal. People danced like they were burning from the inside out, shedding whatever skin the daylight forced them into.

It wasn't an escape.

It was a transformation.

The fog was thicker, the lights sharper, the crowd hotter, sweatier, more dangerous. I felt myself dissolving into the room, the music stripping away whatever still tied me to the suburbs. In the darkness and shadows of the underground was a world without rules, where you could have something—and sometimes too much of everything.

Looking back, I can see it clearly:

Heaven welcomed me.

Powertools tested me.

The night was beginning to train me.

I didn't know then how far it would take me, or who it would turn me into. All I knew was that each new door I walked through felt like a step toward the person built on platform shoes and glitter, made for the spotlight and the neon glow—or maybe the person I had always been, waiting to be recognized.

One night, a flier led us to a warehouse rave that never actually started. When we arrived, a giant piece of plywood leaned against the wall, painted with the names of three clubs and their addresses—Powertools, Some, and a third I can't remember—but no instructions, no explanation. We stood there confused until someone burst out of the darkness screaming, "Club Some is still open!"

And just like that, we were off—tires screeching, hearts pounding, chasing the echo of bass through the Houston night.

Club Some was an after-hours sanctuary, a place where the city funneled itself after last call. Only four clubs in Houston had grandfathered permits to operate after 2 a.m.: Rich's uptown, Some and Numbers in midtown, Powertools downtown, and Tantra off Richmond. Each had its own soul, but some, Heaven and Powertools, had teeth.

The moment we stepped inside, the air hit us like a humid wave of sweat, perfume, and electricity. It was smaller than Heaven, darker than Powertools, infinitely wilder than either. There were no clocks, no expectations, no pretense. People were sweating through their shirts, through their makeup, through whatever daylight identity they'd worn hours before.

No rules.

No curfews.

No shame.

Just sound and possibility.

Max from the east side and his rave crew found us almost immediately—neon bracelets stacked to their elbows, ring pops wedged into their mouths, pupils blown wide open. They moved as a unit, chaotic and joyful.

Upstairs, rows of booths overlooked the dance floor like thrones. One smaller room had walls entirely covered in fur, pulsing under an old-school projector that threw colors across the bodies inside. It felt like stepping into a heartbeat.

At some point in the night, someone cracked a glow stick and smeared the neon goo across their skin, glowing like a radioactive angel. No one blinked. Being inside a nightclub with a group of dedicated ravers was a world where nothing was too much.

As dawn crept in, I pressed my back against a wall, exhausted, ecstatic, watching the entire room blur. And in that moment, a thought bloomed inside me, quiet and confident:

This is it.

This is what I've been chasing without knowing it.

The night had claimed me, and I had no desire to fight it.

A few weeks later, another rave pulled us to the edge of the city—to an abandoned warehouse called The Hangar. It sat under a sky so dark it felt bottomless. But inside, the place exploded with life. The bass was so deep it felt like joy cracking through your rib cage. People wore glitter in their hair, neon beads, and surgical masks.

From a catwalk above the crowd, I watched hundreds of bodies moving as one—lights bouncing off their skin, sweat shining like lacquer. The music wasn't something you listened to; it was something you *became.*

If Heaven introduced me to freedom, The Hangar baptized me in it.

Houston was a ghost town in those days—entire blocks boarded up from the crash of the early 1980s. Downtown was so empty at night that tumbleweeds rolled through the streets. But inside the warehouses, it was tribal, alive, a secret city within a city.

Girls wore pigtails and candy bracelets. Boys wore gym shorts and pacifiers. Whistles echoed back and forth across the dance floor in perfect rhythm. Crews formed—the Matrix Crew, Goodvibe Tribe, the Scooby-Doo Crew— tiny families built from chaos and color.

At Therapy—an old pharmacy turned club—the slick wooden floors thumped under platform shoes. Local club kid icons like David Ra, Darla Dingle, and Bobaysha ruled the room, bending gender and expectations.

* * *

After a few weeks, Roxy's younger sister, Angie, finally cornered us. She was curious—too curious to ignore the stories about where we disappeared to on Friday nights.

She was fifteen, bright, and relentless in her questioning. Eventually, Roxy caved.

"Fine," she said. "But you're staying close to me the whole night."

I nicknamed her Angiosperm—after the flowering plants—because she was always blooming with questions, sprouting new ideas, growing faster than anyone could keep up with. The name stuck.

The night we took Angie to her first rave, we promised Roxy's mom we'd keep her safe. What we didn't mention was that Roxy, Keith (Roxy's boyfriend), and I were all tripping.

Angie was wide-eyed the entire night—watching the lights, the dancers, the DJs. She stayed close, just like Roxy demanded, but her face was glowing with the discovery of something she'd only heard whispers about.

By 4 a.m., we were back at their mom's house, thinking we'd made it home free. We collapsed in the living room—Roxy, Keith, Angie, and me—still buzzing, still seeing tracers in the corners of our vision, trying desperately to act normal.

That's when the hallway light clicked on.

Roxy's mom appeared in the doorway, hair in curlers, bathrobe cinched tight. She took one look at the four of us—pupils like saucers, trying not to smile, failing miserably—and her face shifted from confusion to recognition to something that looked like exhausted resignation.

She stood there for a long moment, arms crossed. Then she said it:

"No more Nice Mommy."

And she walked back down the hallway.

We waited until we heard her bedroom door close. Then we lost it—laughing so hard we couldn't breathe, tears streaming, trying to stay quiet but failing. The phrase became our code, our inside joke, our rallying cry whenever anyone pushed the limits too far.

For years, whenever someone suggested something reckless, someone else would say it: "No more Nice Mommy." And we'd know exactly what it meant.

Houston was a contradiction—silent above ground, throbbing below it. And every weekend felt like an initiation. Heaven was my introduction. The underground club Powertools would be my first test, and the site of my last. The Hangar was my stamp of approval and connection to the past. Club Some was my calling and home away from home. Therapy was my awakening.

And the night?

The night was becoming my destiny.

* * *

It was also around this time that I started learning about the origins of the club kids—not the Houston scene I was growing up in, but the New York movement that would eventually shape the entire country's nightlife. In the early 1980s, a group of eccentric, unfiltered, brilliantly strange artists emerged from the youth of Manhattan—people who dressed like walking sculptures, who lived like performance art, who shattered every expectation of gender, glamour, and identity.

Michael Alig.

James St. James.

Amanda Lepore

Astro Erle

Joey Arias

The names floated through clubs like myths. They ruled Limelight and The Tunnel, transforming nightclubs into runways, and runways into fantasies. They were loud, outrageous, and 100 percent themselves—the purest expression of nightlife as art.

I didn't know it then, but one day I would walk through The Tunnel myself. I would meet the very people who invented the world I was stepping into— legends like Richie Rich, Lady Bunny, Mecca—the original club kids whose names echoed through every city's underground scene.

Back then, in Houston, I only understood fragments of their influence. But even before I knew the whole history, I could feel the connection. What I was witnessing wasn't isolated. It wasn't random. It was part of a larger cultural movement—a living story that stretched from New York to Houston, Chicago, Miami, and LA.

And somehow, without meaning to, I had walked straight into it.

Maybe that's why Heaven felt like home the first night I stepped inside. Perhaps that's why Powertools shook something awake in me. Why Club Some felt like the center of a universe I didn't know existed. Why The Hangar cracked my rib cage open and poured in the kind of joy that leaves a permanent stain.

Maybe the night recognized something in me long before I recognized it in myself. Maybe the night had been waiting.

Houston in those years was a city split in two—sunlight for the workers, moonlight for the dreamers. There was no Internet, no GPS, no online invites. If you wanted to find the next party, you learned to trust your instinct. You follow the glow of distant lights bouncing off warehouse windows. You learned to listen for the faint thump of bass blocks away. Some nights we drove for hours through empty streets, trying to catch a rhythm only the night could teach us. And every time, when we finally found it, it felt like being chosen all over again. Every weekend was another initiation.

I didn't know it yet, but these were the first steps toward an identity that would continue evolving for decades. I didn't know that one day I'd climb the ranks of nightlife, that I'd become part of a world I once only admired from the dance floor. I didn't know that a decade later I would become someone else entirely—a name whispered across rooms, a presence that carried weight, a story people would tell long after the lights came up.

Back then, I was just a kid with a fake ID, a crappy car, and a heart that beat in sync with bass.

But the night had plans.

The night was patient.

It didn't take me all at once.

It claimed me slowly.

Room by room.

Beat by beat.

Club by club.

Door by door.

And from that first night inside Heaven—the night the bass hit my bones; the night TJ glittered like a secret; the night Cheryl screamed with joy beside me—I belonged to it.

I didn't rise into the scene.

I didn't stumble into it.

I didn't get invited in.

The night found me.

And once it did, it never let me go.

* * *

Then, one late night in October 1996, I turned on the TV and stumbled onto an episode of *The Jenny Jones Show*. The topic: Club Kids.

Michael Alig.

James St. James.

Amanda Lepore.

Joey Arias

Astro Erle

Legends dripping in latex and glitter, faces painted like living canvases. They weren't characters—they were worlds. They weren't impersonating art—they were art. Watching them, something inside me detonated.

That feeling returned—the one I'd felt watching *Truth or Dare.* The one who said, "This is you." The one who said, "Stop hiding."

I dug even deeper, remembering Madonna's *Bedtime Stories* performance at Webster Hall—live on MTV—the blue hair, the surreal haze, the feeling of watching someone surrender completely to their own creation.

I wanted that.

Not fame. Not attention. But that level of truth. So I did what anyone on the verge of becoming someone else does:

I went shopping.

I found a pair of 1970s platform shoes at "Wear It Again Sam" in Montrose. They weren't covered in glitter yet—but they would be. I spent hours in my room coating them until they shone like disco balls.

From my grandfather's closet, I borrowed a cream-colored 1950s golfing jumpsuit—a one-piece that clung a little too tightly. On anyone else, it would have looked absurd. On me, it was the beginning of a myth.

I still had my makeup from my old clowning days as Do Nut.. White grease paint. Color pots. Brushes. Tools that once created innocence would now shape something entirely different.

Then I drove to Home Depot—a future temple for my creativity—and bought gray pipe insulation and a silver drainpipe ring. Industrial chic before I knew that was even a thing.

I wrapped the foam around my legs and fastened it with bungee cords. I took a metal dryer ring and taped black nylon letters across it, spelling out a name that suddenly felt inevitable: GHOST.

My face became the final touch—a white base, a black spiral on my right cheek, a lightning bolt slashing across the left—the spiral: the universal sign of life, creation, movement. The bolt: a curse mark and a blessing, Harry Potter meets a hurricane.

When I looked in the mirror, for the first time in my life, I didn't see Mark anymore. I saw something untouchable. I saw someone who could walk into any room and change it. I saw a version of myself I had always been building toward.

I saw Ghost.

I waited until after midnight—the unspoken rule of nightlife—and drove to Rich's on San Jacinto, Houston's legendary club. Even today, some version of it still exists, but back then, it was more than a club: it was a portal.

When I walked inside, everything stopped.

Heads turned.

Eyes widened.

People whispered.

The room shifted around me like I had warped gravity. For the first time in my life, I wasn't invisible. I wasn't trying to blend in. I was the spectacle. And for once, it didn't terrify me. It electrified me.

By the time the crowd began migrating to Club Some, I didn't follow quietly. I entered like someone worth noticing.

Later, at the bar, a couple pulled me aside.

"We love your look," the guy said. "Way more original than that goth thing Munday does. And you're nicer—you actually smile."

It was a small compliment, but it hit like thunder. Validation, from people who lived in the world I'd admired from afar.

By sunrise, the lightning bolt had faded, the spiral had blurred, the glitter had melted into sweat.

But Ghost remained.

I had arrived.

* * *

Looking back now, I can see how perfectly the timeline fits together—like fate connected the dots long before I learned to read the pattern.

The first rave.

The first performance.

The first brush with danger.

The first rescue.

Dallas wasn't just a chapter.

It was radiation.

A chemical vat.

A radioactive spider bite.

The spark before ignition.

Dallas didn't break me—it forged me. It taught me that transformation is never painless, but always powerful. Ghost wasn't born in Houston's Heaven. He wasn't born inside a club at all. He was born in the smoke and chaos of a freezing Dallas warehouse, between a laugh, a pill, a name whispered by a friend, a broken car window, and the beating heart of a night that refused to let me disappear.

From that moment forward, I wasn't just chasing the music. I was becoming it.

And Ghost—once just a joke—became the lens through which I would rewrite my entire life.

II

Discovery

Houston, 1996–7. Ghost wasn't a costume—he was somebody. He learned from legends, found his tribe at after-hours, and lived the Three P's––the perfect party, the perfect pill, and the perfect people. He met Tori, survived an eighty-car crash, and commanded every room. But friends vanished. The scene hollowed out. The persona consumed the person. Then Miami called: Versace murdered, scene shattered, three players rebuilding. They needed Ghost. Houston was conquered. Miami was waiting.

4

Ghost Adventures

Six months after my debut at Rich's, Ghost had evolved from a joke to an identity. Nineteen ninety-six was close to an end.

Not long after I first dressed as Ghost, I saw a flier for a rave at a former Kmart in southwest Houston near South Main—about an hour's drive from Channelview. I stood in line wearing my platform shoes and my signature face paint.

When I arrived at the entrance, I stopped cold. Three of my cousins were working the door—JP, Brandon, and Jana. I would later find out that Jana had married into a family that hosted these parties, and suddenly my secret nightlife collided with my day-to-day world.

Inside, I ran into more familiar faces: Philip V from high school, and my cousin Charity—the former Miss Texas—dancing like the world outside didn't exist.

That night, I learned what people meant by the "dance-floor mentality." The CEO danced next to the sex worker, the lawyer next to the bartender. Society's barriers dissolved under the strobes. Everyone was just bodies moving to the same beat. This venue is the setting at the beginning of my story; it will reappear later at the end, with a haunting conclusion.

I channeled Michael Alig one night when a group of us decided to take our club kid aesthetic into the most mundane space we could think of: Hypermart, one of the four test-market stores, this one on Westheimer Street in Houston, that would eventually become what we now know as Super Walmarts. It was a 24-hour store, which meant we could show up at 2 a.m. dressed like we'd escaped from a rave and treat the fluorescent-lit aisles like our own private runway. Michael Alig had pioneered this in New York—guerrilla performance art that brought club culture into grocery stores, subways, and anywhere "normal" people weren't expecting it. The shock was the point.

I dressed in a blue Walmart employee vest I'd found at a thrift store, white makeup with my trademark spiral and lightning bolt on my cheeks, a blue knitted beanie, and JNCO jeans. We wandered the store as if we belonged there—posing in the frozen-food aisle, dancing past the checkout lanes, turning shopping into theater. Management did not appreciate the performance. They chased me through the store, demanding the vest back, insisting it was Walmart property and I was impersonating an employee. I kept moving, kept performing, until they finally cornered me at the exit. "The vest," the manager said, hand extended. I looked him dead in the eye, smiled, and walked out. I kept the vest. But I never went back to the Hypermart dressed like that again. The point had been made. Club culture didn't need a club—it just needed people brave enough to bring it wherever they went.

* * *

During this time, I lived according to a new philosophy: the Three P's. It wasn't just a joke; it was a way to live in the moment—to chase pleasure, chaos, and attention, and to push the boundaries of what a night could be. The words made people laugh, made them look twice, and sometimes made them wary—but they defined my nights.

The rave scene had Peace, Love, Unity, Respect. But Ghost wasn't born from PLUR. He was born in its shadow, where beauty and ruin held hands. He was born from its mirror—the part of the night that glimmered darker, sharper, and more dangerous, where style was survival.

If the ravers were chasing light, the club kids were chasing shadow.

After the clubs closed, the real adventure began—in dim apartments off Montrose, in whispered invitations, in the liminal space between one song ending and the next beginning.

I had created a mantra to go along with the Three P's. My way of describing after-hours happenings or the dynamics—the strange social choreography--that defined every night: Cling-Ons, Add-Ons, and Roll-Ons.

The Cling-Ons, who couldn't go anywhere alone and latched onto whoever had the spotlight.

The Add-Ons, who arrived with the Cling-Ons and were most likely not actually invited along but came anyway.

And the Roll-Ons, the reluctant drivers who ferried everyone around until they peeled away, leaving the others stranded at dawn.

It was hilarious and tragic all at once—the endless rhythm of appearances and disappearances, people orbiting each other like comets that never collided.

* * *

By the time 1997 came around, Houston's nightlife had begun to change—and so had I. The city still pulsed with music, but I could feel the current shifting east, toward the palm trees and pastel sunsets of South Beach, Miami.

I was ready to chase it.

Ghost wasn't finished. He was evolving.

From Heaven to Fire

By day, I was a manager at Denny's, pouring coffee for strangers under fluorescent lights that made everything look tired. I was able to save up enough money to buy a 1990 Nissan Sentra to ferry me back and forth to work and the nightclubs. I wore a uniform, smiled on cue, counted change, and played the part of Someone Ordinary. But the glitter never fully came off. Even when I scrubbed my hands, specks would catch the light—small reminders of the other world waiting for me after dark.

By night, I was Ghost—painted, shimmering, unstoppable.

It was a double life––two universes sharing one body.

When the clubs closed, the real adventure began.

That was where Ghost truly lived. The after-hours world had its own rules, its own hierarchy, its own gatekeepers. And I was trying to prove I belonged.

Before I left Houston for good, I was still orbiting the familiar landmarks: Heaven, Rich's, Numbers. But each night, they felt smaller. The world I wanted—the world of big lights, bigger risks, and people who lived like art—was somewhere else.

One of the traditions at Heaven: whenever Dee-Lite's "Groove Is in the Heart" came on, every club kid in the building would run to the dance floor—platform converse or T.U.K. shoes pounding, Kikwear jeans and vinyl pants flashing under strobes. During that track, we moved as one. (Years later, in New York, I'd meet Lady Miss Kier herself.)

The after-hours scene was where Houston's nightlife truly came alive. Apartments, Condominiums, and warehouses that were just blocks from Heaven turned into sanctuaries—smoky, chaotic places where friends, strangers, and street kids melted into one pulsing ecosystem. Wigs and boas lay tangled on the floor beside ashtrays and empty bottles. There was always laughter, always drama, always a story being written.

It was during these long nights that I reconnected with familiar faces—TJ, Anson, Star, and Boy Wonder—each one a teacher in their own way.

* * *

By now, I had met Jennifer Silvana, the person we all agreed was the big sister or protector of the local youth, many of whom were homeless and rejected by their true families, and those who identified as, or were seen to be, club kids. Her apartment had become our headquarters—a revolving door of local club kids, ravers, and traveling performers. The walls seemed to breathe with the sounds of laughter, bass, and late-night confessions.

Every night, there was a new argument, a new bond, a new piece of mythology forming. Jennifer's apartment was the epicenter—just a few blocks from Heaven, in the heart of Montrose. People came and went at all hours: club kids, ravers, drag queens, street kids. It was always seamless drama there. Jennifer was granted the freedoms of a trust fund and was always keen to help others in need. Kind-hearted and exploring the party scene in her early twenties, like many of us.

That's where I met most of the Houston club kids. First, there was Wallpaper, who was like the court jester of the club kids, seemingly constantly applying eyeshadow, glitter, or makeup, and dressed in a very haute couture style. Next, Star, the short-haired, extremely tall one, who presented just as her name suggests, always with a smile and looking like a star. Finally, there was Travis, also known as Boy Wonder, who I always felt was one of the leaders of the Houston club kids——a young, dark-haired, handsome gay guy who was always welcoming to me.

Everyone was striving to express themselves, to find their best version, to achieve what we called "third-eye awareness"—the state of consciousness in which one sees beyond this reality to outside forces that influence our being, becoming something greater than themselves through style, performance, and transformation. One night, I showed up at Jennifer's and found a handwritten note taped to the door:

DO NOT KNOCK. DO NOT ENTER. PROPERTY UNDER WATCH.

Too much traffic had drawn attention from neighbors. The apartment manager had warned Jennifer.

I knocked anyway.

Wallpaper opened the door and glared down at me. "You can't be here right now."

"Please let me in," I said. "I want to be part of what's going on."

"Nothing is going on." He looked me up and down, with one eyebrow raised. "Especially not for a newbie like you."

I was still becoming part of the crew, but I wasn't officially one yet.

Then Little Jeff appeared—blond, cute, unmistakably a twink. "Hey, he is one of us. Let him in."

Wallpaper stepped aside.

I'll never forget that moment—finally feeling accepted into this very exclusive subculture.

***

Someone had "liberated" a strobe lamp from a club and set it on the kitchen counter. Every few seconds, it would flash across the room, freezing us all in place like characters from a dream. TJ sat cross-legged on the floor, chain-smoking, wearing a ripped "Heaven" tank top that sparkled under the light. Star was sprawled across the couch, boots on the armrest, lipstick smeared and perfect at the same time. Boy Wonder was holding court in the corner, recounting some half-true story about sneaking into an Erasure after-party. When the beat dropped—some underground mix of Crystal Waters—Anson (Sassy Psycho Bitch) stood up, lifted a bottle of cheap champagne, and shouted, "To those who are too much, too loud, too soon, and too real!"

We all cheered, half in irony, half in reverence.

I stood there, back pressed against the wall, trying to look casual while my heart hammered. This was it—the inner circle I'd been chasing since Dallas. Wallpaper ignored me the rest of the night, but it didn't matter. I was in. Ghost was in.

TJ and Anson were lovers—Gender Bender and Sassy Psycho Bitch, their club kid names as much a part of their identity as their real ones. TJ, tall and glittering, bent gender the way RuPaul did—fearlessly, fluidly, making masculinity and femininity feel like costumes you could wear depending on your mood. Some nights he was pure androgyny, other nights he leaned hard into the feminine side, towering in platforms and painted to the gods.

Anson—Sassy Psycho Bitch—was extremely tall, sharp, all edges and wit. Creative in everything he touched, sassy in every word he spoke. As it turned out, he was from the east side too, from Baytown, even further out than my Channelview. We were both kids from the industrial outskirts who'd found our way to the glittering center.

Around 4 a.m., TJ offered me a cigarette. I didn't smoke, but I took it anyway.

"You're learning," he said, exhaling smoke that caught the strobe. "Rule number one: never look like you need to be here. Act as if the room needs you."

Anson leaned over from the couch. "Rule number two: a real club kid never pays for party favors. Your name is your currency."

TJ nodded. "And rule number three: never show up before midnight."

I took a drag, coughed, tried to play it cool. They both laughed—not at me, but with me.

I never forgot those rules.

Through it all, I found my power in performance—not the kind that required a stage, but the kind that made an entire room turn to look. Every time someone whispered "There's Ghost," I felt that electric recognition. Not for who I was, but for what I had created.

Ghost had a presence—distilled, deliberate, and untouchable.

And yet, even then, I knew there was something bigger happening around me. Rivalries came with the territory. And the club kid who went by Munday and I did not see eye to eye. Back then, we were still at odds. After dancing to Michael DeGrace at club some one night when he featured Jean-Michel Jarre's "Oxygène, Pt. 4," I was sweating and soaking wet. When the song slowed down, I ran over to Munday and gave him a big hug, but he pushed me away and called me crazy. Munday, goth-leaning and territorial, made it clear there was room for only one Eye of Providence at the top of Houston's club kid pyramid. But I didn't need to fight for attention anymore.

Ghost already had it.

The persona was evolving. Every night, a little louder. Every look, a little bolder. Every entrance, a little later.

Through these nights, I discovered the intoxicating power of identity.

Ghost wasn't a costume or a mask—he was energy, movement, and magnetism. He was the echo in the room when the music stopped. Whether it was a crowded after-hours party, a rave in a warehouse, or the corner of a Galleria penthouse, Ghost was always there—electric, unbothered, and unforgettable.

By the end of those nights, the world felt both infinite and intimate. I was no longer sneaking into clubs or following friends.

I was *somebody*.

And somewhere deep inside, I knew this was only the beginning—the prelude to a much larger story.

* * *

You see, during this time, I began to learn more about the original club kids—who they were, and what they stood for. Names like Richie Rich, Walt-Paper, Angel, RuPaul, Lady Bunny, Hedda Lettuce, Amanda Lepore, Keoki, and my personal favorite for their style, Joey Arias. As I would later learn from Superstar DJ Keoki, many of the original club kids were designers, makeup artists, and music students—artists whose rebellion wasn't against society, but against limitation itself. Their world was performance art come to life—fluid, fearless, and unapologetically outrageous.

Ironically, the time when I was beginning my own life as a club kid—1995 to 1996—was the very end of the original movement in New York. According to Michael Musto of the *Village Voice*, this period marked "the beginning of the end" for the original club kid era—the fading of a scene that had once defined the cutting edge of nightlife culture.

But in Houston, the glow still lingered.

And Ghost—born from the echo of a dying movement—was beginning to rise. After that night at Jennifer's, the doors stayed open. But with access came excess—and I'd never been good at knowing when to stop.

* * *

In the Montrose area, several nightclubs had evolved over the years. Heaven was the mainspring, but there was also STEAM—an all-day after-hours that operated differently from Some, which was the after-hours where gay and straight people danced alike. STEAM was pure underground.

The club was housed in an old two-story building. One that looked like it had survived a war. Worn, tattered, held together by music and willpower. Downstairs: a bar, a patio, and a dance floor with an old closet converted into a DJ booth. The building had previously been Mother's, a gay nightclub that had closed years before, and you could still feel that history in the walls—decades of sweat, smoke, and secrets soaked into the wood.

Andy—one of the twin bartenders from Heaven—invited me one Saturday night that bled into Sunday morning.

"Come to STEAM," he said. "It's different. You'll see."

By the time I arrived, it was 8 a.m. I'd been up since Friday night. The sun was already climbing, and most of the city was waking up to church bells and brunch plans.

But inside STEAM, the night refused to end.

That's where I met Mikie Pratt—Meow Meow to anyone who knew him.

He was at the DJ booth upstairs, headphones around his neck, flipping through records with the kind of focus that made everything else disappear. Even from across the room, you could tell he was different from the rest of us. Older, maybe thirty. Extremely well-built—muscular, defined, the kind of body that came from hours in the gym and hours on the dance floor. He spent part of his time as a go-go dancer at the local gay bars and the rest spinning records that could make a room forget time existed.

Mikie had this energy—generous, manic, alive. He'd shout sayings across the booth, keep you laughing with shenanigans, pull you into conversations that felt like they'd been happening for hours, even if you'd just met. He was the kind of person who made you feel like the most interesting person in the room, even when you knew that he could make anyone feel that way.

I walked up during a track transition——when one song ends, and another begins.

"You're Ghost," he said without looking up.

"Yeah."

"Heard about you. Kid painting his face white, making a scene." He glanced at me, eyes sharp but not unkind. "Causing trouble."

I didn't know if it was a compliment or a warning. "That's the idea."

He grinned. "Good. The scene needs trouble. Keeps it honest."

He pulled another record.

Held it up to the light, observing some unseen element as if he were reading something written in the grooves.

"How long have you been doing this?" he asked.

"About a year. Since '96."

Mikie nodded slowly, setting the needle down. Bass flooded the room—deep, hypnotic, pulling the handful of remaining dancers back to the floor like a tide.

"That's about when it ended in New York," he said. "The real club kid thing. Alig went too far. Scene collapsed. Everyone scattered." He leaned back against the booth. "But you wouldn't know about that yet."

"I've heard stories," I said. "About Limelight. The Tunnel. All of it."

"Stories don't do it justice." He lit a cigarette and offered me one. I shook my head. "It was beautiful while it lasted. Pure chaos. Pure art. But chaos burns itself out if you're not careful."

"You were part of it?" I asked.

"LA, mostly. Worked with Trent Reznor early on—Nine Inch Nails, before they exploded. Back when it was just noise and rage in a studio nobody wanted to rent to us."

"What was that like?"

Mikie took a long puff of his cigarette and then exhaled slowly. "Intense. Brilliant. Destructive. Trent knew exactly what he wanted to create, even if it meant destroying himself to get there. He'd work for days without sleeping, push until something broke—the music, the equipment, himself. Didn't matter." He looked at me. "Kind of like what you're doing, yeah?"

I laughed, but it came out hollow. "I'm just trying to have fun."

"That's what everyone says." He turned back to his records. "Until fun turns into something else."

The comment landed harder than I wanted to admit.

Mikie's set ended around 10 a.m. Sunlight poured through the windows like an accusation, exposing every crack in the walls, every stain on the floor, every exhausted face still pretending the night wasn't over.

I walked out into a Houston morning that felt too bright, too real, too close.

The night had been my sanctuary. Now it felt like a cage I'd built myself.

I thought: *Maybe this is what Heaven really looks like—a room full of sinners waiting for sunrise.*

Friends had vanished. Some drifted away quietly, pulled by obligations or other lives. Others burned brightly and disappeared suddenly, swallowed by drugs or the allure of new scenes elsewhere.

Apartments that once overflowed with laughter grew silent. Fliers for parties that used to pack rooms now fluttered forgotten on telephone poles. Even the air felt thinner, as if the city itself were exhaling the last breath of a scene that had once seemed eternal.

Parties began to feel like ghost towns when familiar faces failed to show up. Each disappearance carved another hollow in the world I had known.

Still, I kept going. I kept dancing.

Because that's what Ghost did.

* * *

Ghost was stronger than ever—performing, commanding attention, living for the camera flashes of the popular Polaroids of the day—but the real me was fading fast.

Nights bled into mornings. Mornings dissolved into nothing.

I'd catch my reflection in a club bathroom mirror—white face paint cracked, black spiral smeared—and for a second, I wouldn't recognize the person staring back.

He looked like Someone I once knew.

The thrill that once felt infinite had begun to feel empty, like a song that had played too long. Every party, every high, every performance started to feel like an echo of something I couldn't quite reach anymore.

But still, I couldn't stop.

Ghost couldn't stop.

Because if I took off the makeup, if I stopped showing up, if I wasn't seen—who was I?

Driving home from STEAM one morning, the streets were empty. The neon signs had all gone dark.

My reflection in the rearview mirror looked pale and distant—paint half-gone, glitter clinging stubbornly around my eyes.

It was sunrise, but I was still in the dark.

Mikie's words echoed: "... chaos burns itself out if you're not careful."

Houston was done. Ghost had outgrown it—or maybe burned through it.

Either way, Miami was calling.

And I wasn't coming back.

5

Celebrity, Rave, and Ruin

Eventually, I moved to Coral Hills—everyone called it Crystal Hills due to the excessive presence of stimulant drugs such as MDMA and meth, an apartment complex off Richmond where half the nightlife scene lived. That's where I met Tori.

Tori was an exotic dancer who lived a few apartments away and worked at Solid Platinum, a gentlemen's club in the Heights off TC Jester. She had this energy—dangerous, playful, completely unfiltered—the kind of person who made you feel alive just by being in the room.

One Monday morning after a long weekend of going out, I was crashed on my couch when Tori walked into my apartment without knocking. That's how it was with us—no boundaries, no warnings.

She came straight into my room.

Leaned down.

And kissed me—wet, tongue, aggressive.

I pulled back. "What the—?"

She smiled, pulling away slowly. Saying with a lisp, "Now you're gonna ttttrip ttttoo."

I tasted something bitter melting on my tongue.

"Bart Simpson," she said, laughing. A square of LSD she'd placed in my mouth with the kiss.

"You can't just dose someone!" I said, but I was already laughing too. The absurdity of it, the certainty that the next twelve hours were no longer mine to control.

She sat on the edge of my bed. "Relax. We're going out."

"Where?"

"The Game." She said it as if I should already know.

Twenty minutes later, sitting on my couch, the walls started breathing.

Tori explained the rules while I watched the ceiling ripple like water.

"We hit the bars—straight bars, gay bars, doesn't matter. We see who can pick up the hottest guy. The winner brings him back here. Loser gets to watch ... or join."

I was laughing, not because it was funny, but because the colors were starting to shift, and her voice sounded as if it were coming from underwater.

"I usually win," she added, grinning. "But you get to reap the benefits."

The apartment felt like it was tilting. Music from somewhere down the hall sounded liquid, pouring through the walls.

"We leaving now?" I asked.

"Give it another twenty minutes. Let it really hit."

By the time we walked out the door, Houston looked like a different planet.

Tori drove—I was way too far gone.

We hit a few spots on Richmond—places where the crowd was a mix of curious straight guys, closeted married men, and people like us who didn't care about labels. Tori had an advantage: she was beautiful, confident, and had breasts. Straight guys who wouldn't look twice at me would follow her anywhere.

But I had Ghost.

Even without the full makeup—just eyeliner smudged from the weekend, glitter still clinging to my hair—I had a reputation. People knew the name. That carried weight.

At the second bar, she found him first.

Tall. Dark hair. With the build of a marathon runner. He was standing near the pool table, laughing with friends, completely unaware he'd just become the prize.

Tori leaned in and whispered, "That one."

"He's straight," I said.

She shrugged. "For now."

Twenty minutes later, he was in her car.

I sat in the back seat, watching the streetlights blur into neon rivers, listening to them flirt in the front.

She had already won.

She always won.

* * *

It wasn't long before Tori and I were running the roads together regularly. We mainly frequented the straight after-hours spots—places where curiosity and alcohol made people braver than they'd be in daylight.

There was this handsome guy who lived between my apartment and hers. Tori had been eyeing him for weeks. One night, she convinced him to go out drinking with us.

By the time we got back to my place, the three of us were laughing, buzzed——the recklessness that only happens at 4 a.m. when tomorrow doesn't exist yet.

Tori looked at him, then at me, and said, "Have some fun, just the two of you."

He didn't hesitate. If anything, he seemed aroused by the idea—by Tori watching, by the performance of it all.

I remember her sitting on my bed, legs crossed, eyes bright, thoroughly entertained as he and I ended up in my closet. The irony wasn't lost on me even then—me, still half in the closet in so many ways, having sex with a straight guy in an actual closet while a woman watched from the bed.

He was extremely well-built, confident, and enjoying every second. At one point, Tori called out, "Be gentle with him!"—which made all three of us laugh.

Afterward, he and Tori started dating. They'd go on to make a trip to South

Beach together at some point. I never saw him the same way again—not because anything had changed, but because that night had been so surreal it felt like a hallucination I wasn't sure had actually happened.

That was the rhythm with Tori: work all week at Denny's, pouring coffee under fluorescent lights. Then disappear all weekend into a world where rules didn't exist, where straight guys weren't straight, where a kiss could dose you with LSD, where your closet could become a stage.

By now, Ghost wasn't just a persona—he was a full-blown movement, a mirror-ball reflection of everything Houston's underground wanted to be. The look, the sound, the laughter—it all moved through me like current through wire.

But even electric things burn out if you don't control the flow.

The Three P's: the perfect party, the perfect pill, and the perfect people.

Things had evolved. Now, it was about something more profound—finding the right balance between the chaos and the control.

The night could make you feel immortal, but every glow came with a shadow.

Heaven, Some, and Numbers were still thriving, but the real pulse had shifted. After-hours apartments were packed tighter, raves were wilder, and whispers about "that guy Ghost" began drifting across the city like static. I'd step into a room and feel it—the eyes, the curiosity, the flash of recognition. Ghost had become somebody.

But "somebody" comes with a price. The after-hours world had a rhythm all its own—a cycle that started when most of Houston went to sleep.

Around 2:15 a.m., the first migration began: carloads of dancers, club kids, and dreamers leaving Heaven and Numbers to descend on the hidden sanctuaries.

By 3:00, the music would rise again—slower, deeper, hypnotic—as people sprawled on couches and kitchen floors, glitter melting into sweat. Those nights were full of beauty and madness. They were where you learned who you were—or who you could pretend to be. The apartment parties were laboratories for transformation. Someone was always trying a new look, a new chemical, a new identity. We were scientists of the soul, experimenting with light, sound, and sensation. I remember standing on a balcony one dawn, looking down at the city as the first orange streaks cut through the night sky. But even endless nights have endings. By late 1997, I started seeing the cracks. The Houston scene was changing. What began as a tight-knit circle of club kids at Heaven and Rich's had grown into something bigger—louder, faster, and far less predictable. The city pulsed with a new kind of energy: raves in warehouses, all-night parties in abandoned buildings, and sound systems that rattled the foundations of the Gulf Coast.

By this point, I wasn't just Ghost of Houston—I was Ghost on the move. I had several pairs of one-foot-high custom-made platform tennis shoes and several pairs of seventies-style platform boots. I chased the lights, the music, and the next high across the state. Every weekend was another road trip, another party, another version of the same beautiful entropy.

When I approached the door to Heaven, and even club some now, people knew my name——my presence was expected as a regular patron or clubgoer who had something to offer, but no one really *saw* me anymore. The persona I had built—Ghost—had begun to consume the real me. I was there, but only as a shadow of myself, gliding through the crowd like a ghost——or Ghost——in my own life.

Every weekend, it was the same ritual: dress, paint, glitter, perform. Slip behind the wheel of whatever car I had at the time and drive through the humid Houston night toward the next club, the next party, the next version of myself. The dashboard lights would flicker across my face paint, and in those quiet minutes between parking lots and dance floors, I felt the divide widening—the boy behind the mask retreating further away.

* * *

Even though I now lived in southwest Houston, Heaven still served as my refuge—the place where it had all begun. My bartender there was a twin named Andy Bell, always dressed to kill in Versace. He had a confidence that made him magnetic, and it was through him that I first became aware of Gianni Versace—long before his name became legend.

One night, the club had a crowd of people, the bar humming with its usual mix of regulars and strangers. Out of nowhere, a hush spread through the room, followed by a ripple of excitement. Andy Bell, the singer from Erasure, had just walked in.

He stepped up beside me at the bar, smiled, and said, "You must be Ghost. Could you introduce me to your bartender? He reminds me so much of someone I once loved."

I turned and called my friend over. "Andy," I said, grinning, "meet Andy."

The two laughed, shook hands, and began talking like they'd known each other for years. It wasn't long before they started seeing each other whenever Erasure came through town. Watching them together—one pop icon, one Houston bartender—felt like proof that in our world, the impossible was always just a conversation away.

* * *

Cody, a friend of mine from Dallas who'd moved to Houston, called about the Westheimer Street Festival. The festival was pure Montrose magic—indie shops open, streets closed, techno pumping from Atomic Music where Madam Pussycat and DJ Bizz held court before they defected to form Chemistry Records.

Another day, Daydream—a petite club kid who always wore rainbow everything—loaded into my car for a beach rave hosted by the Scooby-Doo Crew. We walked the sand in our trademark platform shoes and glitter, Cosmic Cat, a founding member of Houston's Scooby-Doo Crew and future House DJ for parties I would throw in the 2000's, and the crew beside us, drawing stares and not caring.

These were the good days—before the crash, before Miami, before Ghost became something I couldn't control.

It was around this time that I began hanging out more and more with Greg, a raver whose obsession with light and sound matched my own. Another irony here: Munday, my archenemy from my early days as a wannabe club kid, had a massive crush on Greg, who did not reciprocate the feelings.

Greg didn't just hear music—he saw it, felt it in colors and patterns. He lived for the pulse--for the split second when the bass dropped, and the crowd became one glowing organism.

Together, we became fixtures of the underground—driving from one rave to the next, sleeping in cars, dancing until sunrise. The highways between Houston, Austin, and Dallas became our arteries. The DJs were our maps.

On one trip to Austin, another club kid—Eric, who went by Shatwika—decided to upstage everyone. They showed up with silver body paint, and by the time we hit the hotel, they had painted their entire body from head to toe.

At first, it was mesmerizing—they looked like a living statue under the fluorescent lights—but within an hour, the room looked like a bomb had gone off at a paint store. Silver handprints streaked the walls, the furniture, the curtains, and even the carpet.

When management came knocking, we tried to act surprised. It didn't work. We were kicked out before sunrise, laughing as we packed our bags, shimmering like disco balls in the hallway.

It was chaos at its purest—absurd, reckless, unforgettable. And because it was the July 4th weekend, the traffic was insane.

The drive home wasn't supposed to be memorable. Greg was behind the wheel, I was wide awake in the seat behind him, and the interstate stretched endlessly ahead. For a stretch of around thirty miles from Schulenburg to Columbus, we had passed a dozen or so wrecks. Each time, the cars would speed up, then all of a sudden slow to a snail's pace again. Cars were bumper-to-bumper until, in a blur of brake lights and screams, everything stopped. I flew forward, my left index finger clipping the back of Greg's headrest. I heard the snap before I felt the pain—a sound like a green branch breaking, sharp and final.

Greg was shouting something. The car had stopped moving. Around us, the interstate had become a graveyard of metal and smoke. Eighty cars, someone would later say. Eighty cars piled up like a child's toys scattered across the asphalt.

I looked down at my hand. The index finger bent at an angle that shouldn't exist.

"Don't move," someone said. A stranger's face appeared in the window. "Ambulance is coming."

I sat there, hand throbbing, watching EMTs move through the wreckage like ghosts themselves. People were crying. Someone was screaming. Greg kept asking if I was okay.

I wasn't.

For the first time since becoming Ghost, I felt fragile. Breakable. Human.

The ambulance ride blurred—sirens, fluorescent lights, a paramedic wrapping my hand. At the hospital, they X-rayed, confirmed the break, and wrapped it in a cast. The doctor said I was lucky. It could have been worse.

But lying in that hospital bed, cast heavy on my lap, I didn't feel lucky. I felt like someone who'd been playing a game without knowing the rules—and just realized the consequences were real.

After being released from the hospital, with a metal brace holding my middle finger in place for healing and taped to my middle hand to secure it in place, I went back to Heaven—because where else would I go? The music was the same, the faces familiar, the lights mercifully dim. Andy, my bartender, saw the cast on my hand and smirked.

"Don't point that thing at me," he said as I lifted my middle finger in mock defiance. I laughed, and for a moment, the pain faded. Ghost had survived—battered, bruised, but still alive, still glowing in the dark. I did not realize at the time, but since I was still partying, my bones did not have a chance to heal, and I still have a bump on my left hand where my knuckle broke.

Raves, mischief, accidents, and hospital visits—they all blurred together into one long neon streak. The music, the danger—they were intoxicating, irresistible. Every crash, every close call felt like proof that I was untouchable.

But somewhere in that endless motion, I started to sense the truth: the world outside the club could be just as wild, just as unpredictable—and sometimes, far less forgiving.

Still, I wasn't ready to slow down. Not yet.

So I drove on—cast, glitter, and all—with the windows down, the bass shaking the frame, and my middle finger raised to the night.

Ghost was still in motion.

Ghost was still riding.

* * *

It was during this time that I met Ted, a fixture in Houston nightlife—sharp, connected, and endlessly curious about people like me. To this day, a mystery person drew Ted and his friends to my style, my nerve, and my ability to navigate the madness without losing composure.

One afternoon, they invited me to their high-rise apartment in the Galleria area. The place looked like it belonged in a movie—sleek lines, white furniture, the faint smell of money and champagne.

And there I was, sitting cross-legged on the floor, unpacking a lunchbox full of McDonald's Happy Meal toys. I laid them out on the carpet, creating a miniature playground while everyone else sipped imported vodka and talked about art and investments.

They watched me, half-amused, half-bewildered. But I wasn't performing—I was being Ghost. I was unapologetically out of place, and that's what made me belong. Sometime during the night, Ted leaned in close. "You should come to Miami with us," he said. "The party never stops down there." He mentioned the players—Big J, Little J, and Yvie —names that meant nothing to me then but would define my next year. "You'd fit right in," he said. "All that glitter and stuff? That's South Beach. That's you."

That was the thing about Ghost: he could exist anywhere.

Then came the call that would change everything. It was Yvie, from Miami. Her voice on the other end of the line was sharp and fast.

"When are you coming down?" she asked.

At the time, I didn't realize how heavy that question was. I had no idea that

Gianni Versace had just been murdered on the steps of his mansion in South Beach—a shock that froze the world of fashion and nightlife.

After the murder, law enforcement cracked down on Miami's party scene hard. Clubs were raided, scenes shattered, and supply lines went silent. Only three major players were left running the underground network—Big J, Little J, and Yvie.

Ted and his circle had connections—and plans. They wanted to help reestablish the flow, and I was to be their envoy, the link between Houston and a South Beach scene trying to rebuild after tragedy.

Suddenly, being Ghost wasn't just about showing up. It was about stepping into a role that blurred glamour, influence, and survival. Houston had been my stage, but Miami would be my proving ground.

I didn't leave Houston right away. There was one more detour—one more festival, one more lesson I needed to learn about what Ghost could become.

Much like Devon, Gary Y, Geary B, and I had met and crushed on a handsome young man named Robert. We had built a rapport and friendship, but it was just that to him, a friendship. While planning my visit to Miami, Robert H called from Shreveport. He had tickets to something called the Zen Festival in Tampa—thousands of ravers converging for three days of music, lights, and transcendence. "Come with me," he said. "Then we'll drive to Miami together."

It sounded simple—a weekend detour on the way to my future.

But nothing with Ghost was ever simple.

The Zen Festival would teach me the difference between being known and being powerful.

Miami was waiting.

But first, I had to learn how to walk into a room of ten thousand people and make them all turn around.

The lesson began in Tampa.

And it would change everything.

But life—or fate, or chaos—rarely lets you move in straight lines.

6

Something to Rave About

After Ted's invitation, the calls started coming.

First from Miami. Ted's voice crackling through long distance, music thumping in the background. "I'm at Little J's place," he said. "Hold on, he wants to talk to you."

Another voice came on the line—higher, faster, electric with energy. "Ghost? Ted's been telling me about you. When are you coming down?"

Little J. The name meant nothing to me then, but his voice carried weight— the kind that came from being connected, from knowing everyone who mattered on South Beach.

"Soon," I said. "I'm working on it."

"Don't work too long," he said, like an invitation and a challenge at once, as if the door were open, but only for those brave enough to walk through it.

A week later, Ted called again—this time from New York. Background noise poured through the line: traffic, horns, voices shouting, the unmistakable chaos of Manhattan.

"I'm with someone you need to meet," he said.

Then another voice. Smooth, amused, knowing. "Ghost from Houston. Ted says you're the real deal."

"This is Cameron," Ted cut in. "He runs half the nightlife in New York. If you ever come up here, he'll take care of you."

Cameron laughed. "Come anytime. We'll show you what a real club looks like."

I didn't know it then, but Cameron was one of the was in the big league—someone whose little black book could open doors I didn't even know existed. His name rang out, etc., in rooms where mine was still a whisper.

"New York's waiting," Ted said. "But Miami first. Get down here. We've got work to do."

Work. The word hung in the air like a promise and a warning.

Ghost wasn't just going to Miami to party.

He was going as a connection.

A bridge.

A player.

* * *

A few weeks later, I met one of Ted's Houston associates in a parking lot off Westheimer.

It was late afternoon––the kind of oppressive Houston heat that made the asphalt shimmer. He pulled up in a black sedan, engine still running. I walked over, casual, like we were just two friends meeting for coffee.

"You good?" he asked.

"Yeah."

He reached into the back seat and pulled out a gym bag. Not heavy, but dense. He handed it through the window.

"Five hundred," he said. "Mixed stamps. Dolphins, Mitsubishis, Stars, and a few Batmans. Don't get caught crossing state lines."

I nodded. I wasn't planning to.

Inside the bag were five hundred ecstasy pills—my currency, my introduction, my ticket into a scene that had been shattered by Versace's murder and rebuilt by the few who knew how to move product without drawing attention.

Ted had made it clear over the phone: I wasn't just going to Miami to show up at parties. I was going to help reestablish the flow. The crackdown after

Versace left a vacuum, and only a handful of people remained to fill it.

Big J, Little J, Yvie—and now, Ghost.

I threw the bag in my trunk, drove home, and stared at it for a long time.

This was different from handing out pills at raves in Houston. This was stepping into a world where the stakes weren't just getting kicked out of a club—they were prison, raids, and federal charges.

But I didn't think about that then.

I thought:

This is power.

This is access.

This is how Ghost becomes more than a costume.

* * *

I called Robert H to say goodbye before leaving for Miami.

We'd been talking on and off for months—the Shreveport crush that never quite landed but never entirely faded either. He had that pull, that energy that made you want to be around him even when you knew it wasn't going anywhere.

"When are you heading down?" he asked.

"Tomorrow. Driving straight through. Houston to Miami, one shot."

There was a pause on the other end of the line. Then, "What if you didn't?"

"What?"

"The Zen Festival. Tampa. This weekend." His voice picked up speed, excited. "Biggest rave Florida's ever seen. Thousands of people. Every major DJ. It's going to be legendary."

I hesitated. I had the pills. I had the plan. Miami was waiting—Ted, Little J, Yvie, the whole scene ready to open its doors.

But something in Robert's voice—possibility, adventure, one last wild moment before everything changed—made me pause.

"Come with me," he said. "Then we'll drive to Miami together. It's barely out of the way."

I looked at the gym bag sitting in the corner of my room.

One detour. What could it hurt?

"Alright," I said. "One stop. Then Miami."

Robert laughed. "One stop. That's all it ever is with you."

He had no idea how right he was.

* * *

The Zen Festival was a living dream—a blur of sound and color stretched across a hundred acres of open land.

We arrived at an outdoor rodeo arena in the Tampa Bay area——the kind of place that usually hosts livestock shows and county fairs. But that weekend, it had become an electronic-music pilgrimage. The entrance, one traditionally reserved for patrons of the yearly rodeo, was lined with orange construction barrels and road barriers. Once you paid and walked through, a young raver girl in butterfly wings handed out flowers to everyone entering.

The excitement was instant, electric. The crowd was pure mid-'90s rave culture—Kikwear jeans, JNCO pants, Adidas sneakers, visors, pacifiers on chains, glow sticks tucked into pockets. Everyone looked ready to dance until the sun came up, then kept going.

Lasers cut through the Florida night. Bodies moved in unison, a living ocean of rhythm and sweat. The ground vibrated with bass so deep it felt like the earth itself was breathing. The air pulsed with euphoria, fog machines, and the collective energy of thousands of people who had traveled from across the country for this.

I'd been to raves before—plenty of them. Houston warehouses, abandoned buildings, underground parties that felt like secrets. But nothing like this.

Zen was a spectacle. A movement. A moment.

And I was about to become part of it.

* * *

It didn't take long to find my people.

I fell in with a group of ravers near one of the main stages—connected, friendly, buzzing with the kind of energy that came from knowing they were part of something bigger. When they found out I had party favors, the vibe shifted. Suddenly, I wasn't just another face in the crowd.

One of them was Jason Donovan, one of the festival's promoters. Tall, confident, moving through the chaos as if he owned it—which, in a way, he did.

"You're the club kid that goes by the name Ghost?" he asked, grinning. "From Houston?"

"Yeah."

"Ted told me about you. Said you might show up." He clapped me on the shoulder. "Come with me."

Before I knew it, I was being ushered into the VIP area and was handed a laminated VIP pass that glittered under the strobes. That single piece of plastic opened every door at Zen—every tent, every backstage lounge, every secret after-party.

I floated through the festival like a specter with access, belonging every-where and nowhere all at once.

In the VIP tent, I met Ziggy Marley—laughing, laid-back, impossibly chill. He nodded at me like we were old friends. Nearby, members of K5 were talking to a group of fans. Their song "Passion" had been a rave anthem for months, and hearing it live later that night felt like the universe aligning.

The VIP pass changed everything. I could move freely, share my pills with people who mattered, and make connections that would follow me to Miami and beyond.

I even let Robert use the pass a few times, slipping him backstage so he could experience the same world I was navigating.

But the night wasn't without its tensions.

* * *

Security and law enforcement were everywhere—more visible than at any rave I'd ever been to. You could feel them watching, waiting for someone to slip up.

At one point, an officer walked straight up to me and ripped the Vicks inhaler off the chain around my neck. I'd melted a safety pin into it so it would hang like a necklace—an everyday rave accessory, something to help with the sensory overload when you were rolling.

"This is illegal now," he said flatly.

I blinked. "It's a Vicks inhaler."

"Doesn't matter—anti-rave laws. Just passed a few weeks ago. You're lucky I'm not searching you."

He walked away, and I stood there, stunned. The scene was changing faster than I could keep up with. What had been normal a month ago was now grounds for arrest.

The night blurred on—music, lights, rain that turned the entrance into a mud pit. At some point, I walked through the parking lot as the sun came up, exhausted and euphoric.

That's when I saw him.

Superstar DJ Keoki, sitting on top of his equipment and record boxes, surrounded by his entourage. He looked untouchable—godlike, even in the harsh morning light.

I'd met him the night before. And that meeting would change everything.

* * *

Earlier that night, backstage at the main stage, I'd found myself face-to-face with DJ Keoki.

He was a legend—the bridge between the New York club kids and the rave scene that had inherited their spirit. He'd played at Limelight, The Tunnel, every major underground party that mattered. His name was regarded in ways I was only beginning to understand.

When he took the stage, everything stopped.

The lights flashed in sync with his movements, illuminating Keoki's face in bursts—godlike, unreachable, commanding. He didn't just play music. He controlled it. Shaped it and made it do things that felt impossible.

Watching him twist beats and bodies with a flick of his hand, I understood what it meant to become more than a person. To become a myth.

Backstage, between sets, I got to talk to him.

"You're Ghost," he said. It wasn't a question.

"Yeah."

"Ted mentioned you. Said you're making moves in Miami."

I nodded, trying to play it cool. "Trying to."

He smiled. "Miami's brutal right now. But if you can survive it, you'll own it. Just don't lose yourself in the process."

I didn't know what he meant then.

But I would.

* * *

Later that night, I ran into the singer from K5 backstage.

She was warm, encouraging, the kind of person who made you feel like your dreams were possible even when the world felt impossible.

"You're heading to Miami?" she asked.

"Yeah. Soon."

"Good. Please do it. Don't wait. Scenes like this—they don't last forever. You have to move while the energy's still there."

We talked about my goals—being a promoter, a club kid, someone who mattered in the world I'd fallen in love with. She told me to chase it, to make it real, not to let fear stop me.

For the first time, I saw a reflection of what Ghost could be—not just a character in the scene, but an energy that others gravitated toward.

On the ride back to the hotel, someone passed around opium. I smoked for the first time, the world softening around the edges, everything feeling distant and close all at once.

It was a festive weekend. A perfect weekend.

And then the world stopped.

* * *

That same weekend, news broke that Princess Diana had been killed in a car crash in Paris.

I didn't find out until later that night, back at the hotel in Tampa. Someone had the TV on in the lobby. The screen showed the wreckage, the tunnel, the bedlam.

The next morning, eating breakfast at the Denny's next to the La Quinta, it settled on me.

A princess died running from the cameras. And we were chasing the spotlight with everything we had. It was a strange mirror—one I didn't fully understand then, but one that would haunt me later.

I didn't realize it at the time, but this was one of the first times I learned the lesson about threes. Gianni Versace. Princess Diana. And soon, Mother Teresa.

Three icons. Three deaths. All within weeks of each other.

The world felt fragile in a way it hadn't before.

I stayed in Tampa for a couple of days, letting it all sink in. Then I drove back to Houston—not through Monroe, Louisiana, like I'd planned. I needed to go home. To think. To prepare.

Miami was still waiting.

But the lesson had already begun.

* * *

By the end of that weekend, meeting celebrities, being sought out, and being made a VIP had opened my eyes to a new world.

I'd seen what power looked like—not just the power of fame or access, but the energy of presence. The ability to shape a room, to shift the air, to make people feel something larger than themselves.

The Zen Festival started as a detour but became a bridge.

It taught me how to blend Ghost's spectacle with purpose. How to move through a scene not just as a participant, but as a force. How to make a laminated pass and a gym bag full of pills open doors that would have stayed locked otherwise.

When I finally left Tampa, I carried more than glitter and memories.

I carried a blueprint.

Houston had made me visible.

Zen made me powerful.

Now it was time to see what Miami would make me.

* * *

I went back to Houston for three days.

Not to stay—to pack, to tie up loose ends, to say goodbye to a city that had made me.

I could no longer keep up with late nights out on the town and early mornings, and I missed one too many shifts, so I was eventually fired from Denny's. No surprise. You can't keep a day job when the night owns you. I'd been bouncing between apartments, crashing with friends, living out of a duffel bag and a trunk full of platform shoes.

Amanda and Chrispix—two friends from the scene—decided to come with me to Miami. Cody, my Dallas friend, mentioned he still had his parents' house in Florida.

"You can crash there if you need to," he said.

We planned to drive in Amanda's car—at least, I think it was hers. The details blur now.

The plan was simple: Houston to Miami via I-10, with a stop in Shreveport to see Robert one more time.

What I didn't know then was that crossing state lines with five hundred pills in my trunk would become part of my story later. Much later. When the consequences of every choice I'd made would come crashing down at once.

But that night, loading the car, saying goodbye to Jennifer Silvana's apartment one last time, watching the Houston skyline shrink in the rearview mirror—I felt invincible.

Ghost was going to Miami.

And Miami had no idea what was coming.

* * *

In Shreveport, plans changed again.

I made contact with some of the people I had met through Robert. One of them, named Ginny, suggested I fly instead of driving. "You'll get there hours before them anyway. Why waste the time?"

It made sense. Amanda, Chrispix, and Cody could take the car and the luggage. I'd fly ahead, meet Ted, and get the lay of the land.

So I bought a one-way ticket to Miami International.

Funny how I only beat them by a few hours.

Funnier still, how that decision—flying instead of driving—might have saved me from getting caught crossing state lines with enough pills to catch a felony.

But I didn't think about that then.

I just thought: *Miami. Finally.*

The flight touched down in the early afternoon.

Sun blazing. The air was thick with humidity and salt. Palm trees swaying outside the terminal windows like they were welcoming me home.

I caught a cab from the airport to South Beach, watching the city unfold through the window—I-95 cutting through downtown, then the causeway opening up to reveal the ocean. The cityscape buildings rose on the horizon, pastel pinks and yellows, impossibly bright against the sky.

It looked like a postcard. Like a dream. Like the place where Ghost was always meant to end up.

Ted had told me he'd be at the Regency Hotel on 9th and Ocean Drive.

When I arrived, he was there with Alecia—sharp, stylish, already moving like she owned the place. I'd maybe met her before at the Galleria high-rise when I was playing with Happy Meal toys on the floor, but this felt like the real introduction.

She looked me up and down, smiled. "So you're Ghost."

"That's me."

"Good," she said. "Because tonight, you're going to Salvation."

I didn't know what that meant yet. But I was about to find out.

Salvation was the world's only weekly circuit party—every Saturday night, from 10 p.m. until 7:00 or 8:00 the next morning. An old warehouse that used to be a fish market, transformed into two stories of sound, light, and sweat. Multiple VIP rooms—music by Junior Vasquez. And every character from the beach showed up, week after week, like church.

Ted grinned. "Welcome to Miami, Ghost."

I looked out at the ocean, at the palm trees, at the neon already starting to glow as the sun dipped toward the horizon.

Houston had been the beginning.

Zen had been the bridge.

But Miami?

Miami was where Ghost would either become a legend—or burn out trying.

The night was beginning.

III

Spotlight

Miami, 1997. Ghost arrived in South Beach with platform shoes and a dream. Within months, he was working the velvet rope at Liquid, one of the most exclusive clubs in America. He danced with celebrities, traveled the circuit from New York to Montreal, and lived the life that once seemed impossible. This is the story of reaching the peak—when the night feels infinite, when you're surrounded by legends, when every door opens and the music never stops. This is Ghost at his highest. Before the fall.

7

First Season

The flight from Shreveport had been short—Ginny beside me, practically vibrating with anticipation. Somewhere on I-95, Cody, Amanda, and Chrispix were still driving the same route I'd just flown over, eating gas-station snacks and blasting music through open windows. We'd all end up at the same destination within hours of each other, but I couldn't wait. Not one more minute.

The moment the plane descended, I pressed my face to the window.

Miami sprawled below like a photo someone had set on fire—turquoise water, white sand, buildings painted in shades of peach and mint and coral that looked like they'd been dipped in sherbet. Everything shimmered. Everything glowed.

The cab ride from the airport was a fever dream.

Art deco facades blurred past—curves and chrome, neon and palm trees, a city designed by someone who believed beauty could save you. The driver had his windows down, and the air that poured in was thick, humid, alive—salt and sunscreen and something electric I couldn't name.

By the time we crossed the causeway into South Beach, I understood what people meant when they said Miami wasn't a city.

It was a drug.

We pulled up to the Regency Hotel at 9th and Ocean Drive, where Ted and Alecia were already waiting on the curb, dressed as they'd just stepped out of a magazine spread—effortlessly expensive, casually untouchable.

Her sunglasses reflected my face at me—white paint, black spiral, eyes wide with hunger.

"So," she said, arms crossed, voice smooth as glass. "You actually came."

"I said I would."

She smiled—sharp, knowing, dangerous.

"Then let's see if you survive it."

That night—my very first night in South Beach—they took me to Salvation.

. . .

Salvation was the church of South Beach nightlife. From the outside, it looked like an old warehouse; inside, it was pure rapture—pulsing beats, shirtless bodies, and light so bright it felt like revelation.

The music hit like a sermon. The DJ was the preacher, the dancers were the choir, and the congregation came dressed in sequins and sin. For the first time since leaving Houston, I felt that familiar hum—the rhythm of belonging, the vibration of being seen.

Ted's circle moved through the tension like professionals—all whispers, favors, and unspoken deals. You didn't ask questions. You just showed up where you were told, said the right things, and never looked too long at what was happening in the corners.

The South Beach elite were ghosts—slipping in and out of VIP lounges, backroom transactions, and poolside mansions where morning light was an unwelcome guest.

But beneath the surface, something was stirring again.

The current was pulling hard, and I could feel it.

That night, I met José, who introduced me to Roy, a local promoter who seemed to know everyone worth knowing.

José, sharp and charming, had a smile that could open any door. Roy, quieter and more observant, watched me with the calculating curiosity of a man who could see potential before anyone else did.

They moved through the club like conductors in command of their orchestra—greeting, laughing, whispering, trading favors in the language of nightlife. They took me under their wing, ushering me into the deeper side of South Beach—the part of the scene where image was currency, and attention was power.

Behind the glamour, behind the lights and the sweat, there was a system—a velvet machine.

Who to flatter, who to avoid.

Who to be seen with.

Who to never mention again.

It was like a ballet.

* * *

After Salvation, José and Roy took me to Twist, another cornerstone of the Beach—smaller, tighter, with a pulse all its own.

Twist wasn't about spectacle; it was about survival.

The crowd was a living mosaic—drag queens, locals, hustlers, tourists—all orbiting each other in a swirl of desire, exhaustion, and ambition.

That's where I met Paloma Picasso—not the designer's namesake, but South Beach royalty in her own right. Paloma was drag incarnate: tall, powdered, and wrapped in charisma that could cut glass. When she entered, the room inhaled. She wasn't just a performer—she was an institution, a keeper of the unspoken codes that held the entire scene together.

When Roy introduced me, she gave me a long, knowing look—that drag-queen smirk, equal parts judgment and blessing.

"Ah," she purred, voice rich as smoke. "So this is the Houston Ghost I've heard about."

I grinned, unsure whether to be flattered or afraid.

She leaned closer, her perfume heavy and intoxicating.

"Miami eats the living and worships the dead, baby," she said, pressing a kiss to my cheek. "You'll fit right in."

And just like that, she drifted away—sequins shimmering like constellations in the dark.

* * *

For the first few weeks, I lived like a true transient, bouncing between hotels on Ocean Drive––first the Regency, then the Holiday Inn. I lived out of my suitcase, chasing parties like they were oxygen.

Days blurred into nights; nights dissolved into pastel mornings that bled over the ocean. I existed in that strange twilight between exhaustion and ecstasy—alive in every sense of the word. In nightclubs—dim lights, loud music, mayhem—I felt at home. I could blend in, perform, disappear at will.

But in intimate situations, I was lost. I couldn't read sexual cues, didn't know when someone was flirting versus just being friendly. So I'd invite people back to my hotel and pull out board games—Twister, Monopoly, anything to avoid the awkwardness of not knowing what they expected. A few weeks later, we were both leaving Liquid around 3 a.m., I asked Paloma if she had plans, and I can remember inviting her back to chill. Paloma dismissed the idea, saying that I threw the "worst" after-parties.

But my social awkwardness wasn't the only problem I was facing.

There were a few power struggles between Ted and me when I first arrived. My crew had trusted me with a couple of hundred ecstasy tabs and had "fronted" around a hundred to José. Ted was livid.

In the higher-numbered streets at the Holiday Inn, a thirty-story high-rise on Collins near 40th Street, Ted confronted me about it. José never came through with the money, and Ted told me that anyone else would hang me out the window by my ankles. I can remember him asking what I saw in José, saying that he was worthless.

As a challenge, and to prove that exact point, Ted handed José another round of a hundred pills to see what he could do with them. I was encouraged to sit and think through my actions in the bathroom. When he did not return after about eight hours, Ted sent me to find him and the supplies. I did not know before this incident, but I definitely knew after that I had to learn a lesson that night: cash up front.

But even dreams need an address.

Eventually, I moved into a two-story apartment at the Commodore Residences on Collins Avenue, blocks from everything that mattered. It wasn't luxury, but it was mine. From the balcony, I could see the city —a neon mirage where glamour and decay shared the same bed.

* * *

By then, I wasn't just a visitor—I was part of the rhythm.

The velvet machine had accepted me as one of its gears.

Thursdays were for the Warsaw Ballroom, hosted by fellow Texan Elaine Lancaster, a queen with a microphone, a martini, and a presence that could fill the entire Beach. She was the one to introduce me to Lady Bunny (a club kid in her own right) for the very first time when she was in town spinning, and one of Lady Bunny's trademarks from back then was grabbing guys' Junk. I was envious.

Fat Back Pussy Cat on Monday nights, Liquid was the temple—the night everyone showed up to worship the music, the moment, and each other. Kitty Meow and Paloma Picasso hosted it, and it was everything Miami wanted to believe about itself.

We started downstairs, singing along to Deborah Cox's "Things Just Ain't the Same" and Ultra Naté's "Free." Those songs weren't just hits—they were hymns. They captured everything we lived for: heartbreak, survival, and the intoxicating illusion of freedom.

Later in the night, we'd migrate upstairs to the mixed VIP lounge, where the air was thick with perfume, power, and possibility.

One Monday, I dug out my oldest and favorite pair of platform shoes— silver, six-inch monsters that made me feel invincible. Halfway through a spin, my heel snapped. I crashed into a table, nearly sending drinks flying into Yvie and her friends.

"Ghost, you idiot!" she shouted, half-laughing, half-scolding. "Watch what you're doing!"

I balanced on one foot, glass still in hand, and smirked.

"It's not a party till something breaks."

She rolled her eyes but smiled—because she knew I was right.

* * *

There was one night that captured it all—Warsaw Ballroom, a cathedral of sweat and light. The humidity wrapped around us like silk, and the crowd moved like waves, crashing against the stage and each other.

Ted was at the bar, sharp suit gleaming. Alecia was on the dance floor, her sequined dress reflecting the strobe in a thousand tiny suns. And I stood in between them—suspended between power and chaos, love and illusion. Kitty was always looking out for people. The time frame of my arrival in South Beach was still the height of the AIDS crisis—PrEP was a decade away—and she took her role as mother hen seriously.

One night at Warsaw, I watched her break up a situation in the upstairs bathroom. Several shirtless twenty-somethings were getting carried away, and Kitty knew one of them was HIV-positive and not using protection.

She didn't make a scene. She just followed the guy down the stairs, her finger pointed like a mother scolding a child.

"You know better," she said firmly. "With your status, you know better."

Always eloquent. Always polite. Always protecting the community, even when no one else was watching.

Years later, Kitty and Paloma would be honored at the White House for their tireless work toward a cure and human rights protections for our community. Moments like that were why.

* * *

A few weeks later, Liquid hosted Paloma's birthday party—one of those nights when every queen, promoter, and misfit flooded the club in a sea of sequins and noise.

I had planned a surprise performance in her honor.

I handed my CD to the DJ——Bugie——who looked it over, sneered, and tossed it back at me.

"I don't play CDs," he said. "Only vinyl."

The rejection stung. Laughter rippled through the crowd—but not for long.

Maricello, Liquid's gatekeeper, sprinted to find Ingrid, one of the owners. She swept in like a storm in heels and demanded, "Let him perform."

Moments later, the lights dimmed, and the Basement Jaxx techno remix of "Sesame Street" burst through the speakers.

Dressed as Big Bird Ghost, I exploded into motion—yellow feathers, golden beak, and boa flying as I fluttered across the dance floor. The crowd howled, cheering as I twirled through the lights, knocking drinks, kissing strangers, owning the chaos.

When the last beat hit, I stood panting in the strobes as gold feathers rained like confetti.

Paloma blew me a kiss from across the room. And as per usual for our interactions, in her long, thick Cuban accent, she sweetly said, "Ghoooost. Best birthday gift ever."

By sunrise, my name was everywhere. "The Big Bird number" became a South Beach legend, and I performed it again—once more at Liquid, then I was asked by Nathan Jodd to dress up and perform for a private party for Veto, for one of South Beach's most well-known promoters. Afterwards, I was invited to join Paloma and the dancers on stage at Salvation for a glitter-drenched rendition of the 5th Dimension's "Let the Sunshine In."

It was this acceptance and being held in high regard by such a legend that made me realize something devastating and straightforward:

Ghost had officially arrived.

* * *

But the higher you fly, the faster you draw fire.

At Salvation, I met Yoko, a fierce, white-painted, Geisha-clad club kid–drag queen hybrid who seemed to float above it all, commanding her own spotlight even among hundreds of shirtless men. She was a vision of control in a world built on frenzy.

That same night, I met Chastity, who would soon become my roommate. We bonded instantly, reckless and radiant, spinning through the scene as though we owned it.

I had hidden a few party favors in gum wrappers and was passing them out to friends—harmless by our standards. But one jealous New York club kid took offense at being left out and ran straight to management. Within minutes, Security guards had me in their hands. I was roughed up and thrown out the side door like a piece of trash.

The Miami air hit me like a slap. I sat on the curb, glitter clinging to my sweat, the bass pounding through the walls. For the first time in a long time, I felt puny—mortal.

A few weeks later, the phone rang. It was Nathan Judd, the leading promoter at Salvation.

"Ghost," he said with a laugh, "come back this Saturday. Let's clean the slate."

When I walked back into Salvation, dressed as Space Cadet Ghost, with silver dryer piping around my neck and an actual TV antenna coming out of my hairdo, Kitty Meow was in the dressing room, perfecting her eyeliner, with Paloma telling her, "You need more." She caught my reflection in the mirror.

"You've got something special," she said. "But baby, you're bringing way too much attention to yourself. In this town, that's not always a good thing."

She was right. In Miami, attention was power—but it could also be a curse.

* * *

On Sunday nights in South Beach, David Knapp was the DJ and one of the nicest people. We met at the outdoor arena off Ocean Drive and 1st Street.

As for the geographic layout, this was at the very beginning of Ocean Drive, a unique part of South Beach. Paloma would tell me about several other clubs in this area back in the day, including a basement club that was no longer running but was a fabulous underground legend among South Beach partiers.

The Sunday night party at Amnesia was promoted and hosted by Connie Casserole, with Pagan (Sexcellia) as the primary host.

Imagine hundreds of shirtless circuit boys dancing out in the open air in the evening, T-dancing on Sunday afternoons, starting in the sunlight and ending with a chill. Connie Casserole, the larger-than-life, Divine drag queen, with some of the most unique outfits on the Beach, including a white face outfit with purple duo puffs, like something out of a cartoon.

I remember one Sunday night, a tourist asked what everyone was on.

I pulled out my knitted hand puppet. Each finger had a different face—my "girls," I called them.

"Meet Tina," I said, wiggling one finger. "She's the dirty one. Use sparingly."

"Kathy gives you superpowers," I continued, moving to the next finger.

The whole VIP lounge cracked up. Someone snapped a photo. Within days, people across South Beach were calling their drugs by Ghost's names—Tina, Molly, Kathy, Gina, Amy.

It was absurd. It was dangerous. It was precisely the kind of thing that made Ghost famous—and made Mark Stevens disappear a little more.

When combined correctly, they made for a magical night. When misused, they could be deadly.

But we didn't think about that then. We just thought about the next party.

I had connections in Houston, and pills flowed through me in waves—hundreds at a time. Batman logos, skull and crossbones, purple horses, blue diamonds, yellow stars. Each pressing had its own reputation, its own flavor.

You never knew exactly what you were getting—everything from pure MDMA to kitchen-sink cocktails—but if you found one that hit right, you grabbed as many as you could.

I even named one of my outfits after them: Lucky Charms Ghost, a play on "magically delicious" and the rainbow of pills circulating through South Beach. An Irish green top hat, Green striped Kikwear jeans, the lucky charms lunchbox, and again the signature lightning bolt and spiral makeup.

8

The Velvet Machine

The season on South Beach and in Miami in general was a living, breathing entity of its own. From the time the rest of the country was beginning to feel the chill, South Beach was revamping, dusting off, and adapting to the fashion world's takeover.

I had the privilege to run the roads with Nathan Judd during one of these planning periods, and we were scouting venues for the next big party on and off the beach.

We were on our way back to the beach from a central condo party, and Nathan spotted a four-story blue building that appeared to be an abandoned warehouse. He immediately asked the cab driver to pull over. We drove around the building, and he took down numbers. A few years later, I would learn that that location had become the nightclub named "Space" and had risen in popularity as an in-between party spot for both those on the beach and those in downtown Miami.

It was a few months into my first season that I realized my previous look was amateur compared to those around me. There was a definite need for a style progression.

I was inspired by the South Beach queens who'd perfected their signatures: Paloma's effortless elegance, Kitty's fierce polish, Connie's divine extravagance. Each had a look so cohesive you could spot them across a crowded club in an instant.

I needed to find mine.

I was shopping at boutiques and had acquired a pair of designer Italian platform shoes. Black and white, maroon, white, and the leopard-print ones that featured in so many future outfits.

One specific thing I noticed about most of these local celebrities was that their club persona and daily self were two entirely separate personas. One night at Liquid, I was dancing when three men surrounded me on the floor. Something about them felt familiar—the way they moved, the confidence— but I couldn't place them.

They were watching me, smirking, like they were in on a joke I wasn't getting.

One leaned in close. "Having a good night, Ghost?"

I nodded, still trying to figure out who they were—good-looking guys, well-dressed, but nobody I recognized from the usual crew.

It wasn't until the next night that I learned the truth: Connie Casserole, Leslie Quick, and Elaine Lancaster—three of the most recognizable drag queens on South Beach—had been standing right in front of me, out of drag, and I hadn't had a clue.

They'd been testing me. Seeing if Ghost could recognize them without the wigs, the makeup, the armor.

I couldn't.

It was a reminder of something important: in South Beach, the persona and the person were two entirely different things. The queens I knew on stage—larger than life, untouchable—were just people during the day. And they kept those worlds separate for a reason.

I'd passed their little test, in a way. I'd treated them like anyone else, because to me, they were just three guys on the dance floor.

But the joke was on me—because they knew exactly who I was.

* * *

I met Matt through the network of club people, around the same time I met Chastity—the night Kitty scolded me for my excessive attention-drawing attire.

Matt was an art student at Miami University who lived in the dorms. He had model looks—blond, shoulder-length hair, tall and clean-cut—and worked at The Body Shop, always talking about healthy skin and natural beauty. He carried a satchel everywhere, filled with sketches and pencils, always creating something.

He was different from the other guys I'd chased on the beach. Matt was steady. Sweet. Safe in a way that felt foreign to me.

We'd meet after his shifts, grab coffee on Lincoln, walk the beach at hours when the party people were finally sleeping. He'd sketch while I talked, filling pages with faces from the clubs, capturing the scene without ever really being consumed by it.

Our physical relationship was … gentle. Not charged with the manic energy I was used to. He wasn't extremely sexual, which confused me at first. I kept waiting for him to want more, to push harder, but that wasn't Matt. He was content just being together.

Looking back, I think he saw me more clearly than I saw myself. He'd watch me get ready for the clubs—the makeup, the platforms, the transformation into Ghost—and sometimes I'd catch this look in his eyes. Not judgment. Concern, maybe. Like he was watching me disappear.

"You don't have to do all this, you know," he said once, gesturing at my reflection.

"Yes, I do," I said.

He didn't argue. He just went back to his sketch.

We lasted a few months before drifting apart. He wanted quiet. I needed volume. He was an artist observing the scene. I was the scene consuming itself.

Years later, I'd understand what he'd been trying to tell me. But back then, I was too busy becoming Ghost to hear it.

* * *

After about a month at the Commodore, I traded the beach views for something closer to the heartbeat—a small apartment just off Washington and 14th Street, only a few blocks from Liquid. From there, you could feel the pulse of South Beach through the walls—basslines thumping, car doors slamming, laughter echoing off stucco at all hours.

It was the perfect move. I was no longer an outsider floating from scene to scene; I was plugged directly into the current. I began to understand how South Beach worked, and what was considered currency was who you knew, not what was in your wallet. My landlord at the apartment off of Washington and 14th was an entrepreneur who saw the dollar signs in my adventures.

It amazed me how anytime I needed anything, he would show up on my doorstep with the answer. Groceries were running low, and he was there with a cart full for $100. No place to sit; he was across the hall in a vacant unit with brand-new sectional and bedroom furniture for $800. Needed a TV, and he was at the door with a brand-new one in the box for $250. Always cash, never any questions.

At one point, he invited me to his apartment to introduce me to a fabulous young lady who was looking for a connection with a good-looking US citizen--someone she could marry and move in with for a small fee.

Later, he would buy back the items slowly and for half of what I paid for them, as the money dried up--as a favor to me, of course.

As you might imagine, especially during the season (when the rest of the country is freezing, but it's still warm and sunny in Florida), the fashion industry arrives en masse in South Beach.

My new apartment came with an entourage of neighbors straight out of a dream. My upstairs neighbor, James, was best friends with Eli. Eli had moved to South Beach with his former partner, and they had started an escort business named "Prestige Entertainment," which had offices in a tower on Lincoln Avenue and Collins.

I would visit the operation on occasion, and the owner--Eli's ex--would switch his voice to answer the phones, going from his own deep voice to female receptionist with ease, saying, "It's cheaper if I do it myself. I know the calls will be handled correctly." At one after-party, we ventured across the bay to central Miami and the condo that Eli's ex and his new partner lived in.

It was here that I saw my very first bidet; it was also another experience in which I felt awkward.

Not being completely in the know about sexual cues, I can remember that after a few hours of the after-party, one guy asked me when we were getting naked and having sex, in front of a room of about a dozen people.

I grabbed my things and called a cab back to the beach.

Upstairs was Chyna Girl, a South Beach icon—a blur of wigs, laughter, and music rehearsals that shook the ceiling. Even her footsteps sounded like applause. She lived with James from Alabama, a good-looking young man who worked as a blackjack dealer on one of the gambling boats that docked in Miami and sailed into international waters to play.

Then there was Dallas, also known as Futura, a fellow club kid and fashion visionary. We clicked immediately—two glitter-fueled spirits spinning in the same orbit. Our afternoons were filled with the hiss of hot glue guns, the shimmer of sequins, and the smell of hairspray thick enough to choke an angel.

There was Leslie Quick, effortlessly cool, and Chastity, androgynous and magnetic—soon to be my roommate and one of the closest people in my Miami life. Together, we made art out of survival. We were the night's architects, crafting our identities piece by piece, outfit by outfit, until the world bent to notice.

Leslie was roommates with Power Infiniti (Ted's favorite) and worked at the shop named POP, where I bought many cool, unique bags, like my Stoplight one and my one-of-a-kind Kabuki backpack, adding a more designer twist to my style.

Matt and Chastity hatched a plan—one of my favorite Miami memories.

Kevin Aviance was throwing a party at the Delano Hotel. Exclusive. Invite-only. The kind of event where security checked names twice and side-eyed anyone who looked out of place.

We decided to crash it.

I showed up dressed as Chester Cheetos Ghost: leopard-print platform shoes, gold shorts, and my stop-and-go backpack slung across my chest. I wandered through the poolside crowd, handing out bags of Cheetos to confused models and celebrities lounging on white deck chairs.

Most people laughed. Some looked annoyed. A few actually ate them.

Then Kevin Aviance himself appeared—towering, radiant, dressed in something that looked like it cost more than my rent. He smiled politely, but his eyes said everything.

"Ghost," he said, voice smooth as silk. "I think it's time for you to go."

"One more?" I asked, holding up a bag of Cheetos.

He raised an eyebrow.

I spotted Veto across the pool and tossed him a bag before Kevin's security could escort me out. Veto caught it, laughing, surrounded by a crew of model-looking guys soaking up the sun.

One of them looked familiar. I'd seen him at the Zen Festival months earlier—and before that, at raves in Austin. The world was smaller than I thought.

Or maybe I was just bigger than I realized.

Either way, I left the Delano with my head high, Cheeto dust on my hands, and another story to tell.

We didn't live in South Beach.

We were South Beach.

* * *

Having taken the advice that Kitty Meow had given me about bringing too much attention to myself, and having been introduced to Dallas's ex-partner, who was one of the seamstresses and designers and a former club kid drag performer themselves, I decided to go all out and prepare a "special," more refined outfit for the upcoming "jungle" weekend. I bounced a few ideas around, and we settled on a green vinyl fabric that glistened like artificial plants found in an office building, and we sewed half a yard into a simple ankle-length skirt.

I then painted a pair of platforms forest green, folded a newspaper into a homecoming-parade-float-style carnation and placed it on my head with some fruit attached, and wore a camo-inspired top to become Carmen Miranda Ghost.

I was thrilled that one of my hairdresser acquaintances during that time agreed to dress up with me and go out. There were jungle-themed events all over town, and we went club-hopping, landing at Salvation, where Kitty grabbed my hand and said, "Well done, this is classy."

One of my favorite looks was Carmen San Diego Ghost—a character so specific that I spent weeks planning every detail.

I found a vintage red trench coat at a consignment shop on Washington, altered it to hit mid-thigh, and paired it with a matching red wide-brimmed hat. Black platforms. Dark sunglasses. A leather satchel slung across my chest like I was carrying stolen artefacts.

The genius was in the details: I printed tiny question marks and pasted them across the coat lining, only visible when it moved. I carried a plastic globe as an accessory. I handed out "clues" on folded paper all night—cryptic messages leading nowhere.

I wore it to Liquid on a Saturday, and the reaction was immediate. People got the reference—Carmen San Diego, the mysterious globe-trotter, always one step ahead. It was perfect for Ghost: elusive, clever, impossible to pin down.

Paloma spotted me across the dance floor and laughed—that deep, knowing laugh that said she approved. "Ghooooost, you are too much," she said, adjusting my hat.

By the end of the night, half the club was asking, "Where in the world is Ghost?"

The answer, of course, was everywhere and nowhere at once. Just like Carmen. Just like the character I was becoming—impossible to catch, even by myself.

* * *

As I integrated more deeply into South Beach nightlife, I met James Cubby, a photographer and journalist for the *Flamingo*, a local paper often displayed on cafe tables alongside *Ocean Drive* magazine. He'd been documenting the scene for years, and I'd appeared in several of his articles as "Ghost of Austin, Texas, Fame."

One afternoon, he asked me to lunch on Lincoln Avenue. We sat at an outdoor table, people-watching as models and tourists drifted past. James spread photos across the table between us—me in different costumes over the past months. Bart Simpson Ghost. Big Bird Ghost. Carmen Miranda Ghost. Green Ghost. A dozen others I'd already half-forgotten.

"You see the problem?" he asked.

I looked at the photos. Each one was bold, colorful, and attention-grabbing. But together, they looked scattered. Chaotic. Like twenty different people trying to be one character.

"You're all over the place," he said, not unkindly. "Ghost needs to be a brand. Cohesive. Recognizable. Right now, you're trying too hard."

I felt defensive. "I'm being creative."

"You're being desperate," he said, and the words landed like a slap.

He leaned back, lighting a cigarette. "You're already known. That's the hard part. Now you need to refine it. Less raver, more Ghost. Pick a direction. Let the persona speak for itself instead of shouting through twenty different costumes."

I stared at the photos—evidence of months spent chasing attention, validation, and belonging.

He was right.

"You want to stay in South Beach?" he asked. "You want to become one of the characters here? Then act as if you belong. Not like you're begging to be noticed."

I nodded slowly as James gathered the photos back into a pile.

Years later, back in Houston, I'd remember this lunch when I became a promoter myself. James Cubby's critique would guide me: focus, cohesion, brand. Less is more.

But that afternoon on Lincoln Avenue, I just thanked him, paid for lunch, and walked back to my apartment—unsure whether I was ready to hear what he was telling me, but knowing deep down that he was absolutely right.

Several other magazines besides the *Flamingo* appeared during this time. One was named *Guy*, and when they launched Sexcillia, Pagan was working there, excited to be helping this new era of queer representation begin.

I remember the founder describing it as a magazine you could leave lying out without friends or family being shocked or embarrassed by the gayness of it all.

I was able to visit the offices, and they had already published three editions.

This publication was glossy and clean, featuring all the local celebrities' nightclubs and being fired up for the upcoming season. South Beach had a way of promoting itself and the characters who lived and worked there.

It was in the early days of the Internet, before podcasts were common, that The Womb, among the world's first online radio stations, was launched. I was invited to the office with "The Womb" in bright pink letters on the entrance wall.

It was a small office with a smaller recording suite, similar to a terrestrial radio setup but with much less equipment.

I spoke with the on-air DJ for a few minutes, who invited me back in a few weeks to be interviewed, and left just as several famous Grammy Award-winning rappers and R&B artists, infamous in today's headlines, were coming in for a radio spot. This entertainer would change his name many times over the years, but I met him when he went by Puffy.

* * *

Not everyone I met in South Beach was a fan of my style or attitude. One of those people was Kevin Crawford, a New Yorker who'd transplanted to Miami to help market and run Liquid. He had a certain disdain for me from the beginning.

One night, I carried a Dymo label printer into the club and started labeling everyone—"Snob," "Cute," whatever I saw. I'd print the label and paste it on people. Kevin abhorred what I was doing.

Not long after, Kevin was fired as the club's entertainment director, which was owned by New Yorkers considered to be inside Madonna's inner circle.

When I ran into him after that, I felt humbled. I apologized for how I'd acted.

Soon after, there were open auditions for talent at Liquid, and I was determined to get hired. My interview came directly after Connie Casserole's. I showed up in full Bart Simpson Ghost—yellow high hair, Bart overalls, yellow platforms, full makeup.

Connie looked at me and said, "Oh, we were supposed to dress up for the interview? My style speaks for itself."

I didn't get hired.

Two weeks later, I walked up to the ropes on the Washington Avenue side of Liquid and saw my neighbor Dallas in costume—a hybrid of Woody and Buzz Lightyear—an outfit I'd planned to create but never finished. Dallas had put it together to perfection: white cow leather, painted face, futuristic ray gun shooting red lasers.

He'd won the position I'd applied for.

And he deserved it.

You see, Dallas worked at Eckerd Drugs in the photo lab department. Dallas was the one person in South Beach who truly knew what went on—because he was the one developing all the photos.

* * *

I had the pleasure of meeting one of Spencer's friends, Ned——who had grown up in New York with Spencer——on an outing to Fort Lauderdale one weekend, hitting the best gay clubs and leather after-hours you could hope for.

Unknown to me at the time, Ned was HIV-positive and dealing with illness due to AIDS. We hit up club after club until all hours, and then I made my way back to the apartment on Washington.

I can remember finding the back door wide open and my safe wide open. Then all of a sudden, the phone rang. It was a call from Yvie warning me to get out of my apartment asap. Something was definitely off, so I immediately went upstairs and out the back emergency exit onto Washington Avenue and headed toward the bay side and Yvie's apartment.

It turned out that Spencer had sent two guys to rough me up because his friend, who had gone out with us, was in the hospital, and Spencer had adamantly informed everyone in Florida not to party with Ned due to his status, which was unknown to me at the time. I exited out my back door and down an alley, disappearing as any good Ghost would.

I went to Yvie's apartment, and once I finally found it, having been on the wrong floor for several hours with a dead cell phone, we straightened things out, and I made peace with Spencer ahead of my New York trip, where I would finally meet Spencer in person.

I had several crushes during my time there. But the biggest crush was a super-chiseled, Cuban, Coral Gables transplant with the rock-hard body of Adonis named Giovanni. He would pronounce my name very similarly to Paloma, long and drawn out: "Ghoooost." I had been chasing him up and down the beach for weeks before I met Matt. But after being turned down multiple times, I finally moved on. Weeks later, late one night, there was a knock at the Washington and 14th apartment.

I opened the door to find Giovanni standing there, sweating, pupils dilated, speaking rapid Spanish mixed with English.

"Ghoooost," he said. "You got anything?"

He was begging for party supplies, desperate in that way people get when they've been up for days and can't find their way down.

Before I could answer, he started stripping—shirt first, then pants, until he was standing naked in my doorway, his body as perfect as I'd imagined during all those weeks of chasing him around Ocean Drive.

"Ghoooost," he said again, stepping closer. "Do you want to suck my dick?"

He said it over and over, like a mantra, like an offer, like a transaction.

I looked at him—this Adonis I'd chased for weeks, now offering me exactly what I'd wanted, but wrong. All wrong. Not desire. Desperation.

"No," I said.

He blinked, confused.

"Get dressed, Giovanni."

I gave him what he came for—the pills, not the sex—and sent him on his way.

The next morning, I thought about that moment when I'd spent weeks wanting something that, when offered, I didn't actually want anymore.

Maybe Matt had been right.

Maybe I didn't always know what I was chasing.

9

Ghost on the Go

Before the next descent came one last glittering high.

My upstairs neighbor, the blackjack dealer James, decided to make the trip back to Houston with me. We even managed to see Ted again before we left, laughing about the nights that never seemed to end.

That weekend at Rich's—the very place where it all began—felt like a coronation. I stood in the center of the dance floor under spinning lights, untouchable, glowing like a true vision from South Beach. My see-through neon green jacket caught every flash. My glitter makeup shimmered perfectly against my cheekbones, and my Kikwear jeans gleamed like something straight off Ocean Drive.

I had returned home transformed—no longer the kid sneaking into Heaven, but Ghost in full form. During this trip, I was able to connect with Dan and Chiara, two individuals who were both connected and strange. Dan was someone who was seemingly addicted to gamma-hydroxybutyric acid (GHB), and Chiara was dedicated to him to the end. We had hung out back in my days at Crystal Hills when I was roommates with Julian. It was Chiara who drove us to the airport and dropped us off, taking an unsuspecting Polaroid of us at the drop-off and wishing us safe travels and farewell. I am not entirely sure, but I think the Polaroid picture at the Houston airport was somehow sent to the DEA in Miami and helped identify James and me when we landed.

When it came time to fly back to Miami, we booked one-way tickets and paid in cash—standard practice for us, though it drew more attention than we realized. At the counter, the airline rep looked us over, then scribbled one strange word on our tickets: "Crayola." I didn't think much of it at the time.

But when we touched down at Miami International, two DEA officers were waiting. They approached calmly, flashed badges, and asked to search our bags. I didn't argue. They rifled through my clothes and pulled out a bottle of GNC "diet pills." I smiled, told them how much weight I'd lost, and even showed them an old photo from two years earlier. They asked if they could keep two of the pills for testing. I laughed and said, "Sure—why not?"

It felt harmless.

Routine.

Nothing to worry about.

But I was wrong.

That moment—that small, forgettable act of compliance—was the beginning of the end.

* * *

On this same trip back to Houston, the promoter Gary James invited me to check out the Spy Club—a venue he'd opened while I'd been building Ghost in Miami. It felt strange being back on Houston turf as a guest instead of a fixture, but Gary had heard about what I was doing in South Beach and wanted to connect.

The Spy Club sat just around the corner from where Powertools used to be—a gritty basement fortress I once visited often. Walking those blocks felt like visiting a past life—one I'd lived so fully I'd almost forgotten what came before it.

Gary waved me into the VIP lounge, where a family was celebrating something—champagne, laughter, the easy energy of people on the verge of something big.

"Ghost," Gary said, pulling me over. "Meet the Hernandez family. They just signed the lease on 709 Franklin."

I blinked. "Powertools?"

"Used to be," one of them said, extending a hand. "We're turning it into something new. The Living Room. Softer vibe, different energy. Pop house, lounge atmosphere. We're done with the industrial dungeon thing."

I looked at them—this family who'd just leased the space where I'd spent so many nights losing myself in the dark.

"The Living Room," I repeated.

They nodded, excited. "Opens in a few months. You should come check it out when you're back in town."

I smiled, shook hands, and congratulated them. Told them I'd love to see what they did with the place.

But standing there in the Spy Club VIP lounge, champagne in hand, I felt the distance between who I'd been and who I was becoming.

Powertools had been a sanctuary for the version of me that needed darkness to feel alive.

The Living Room sounded like something else entirely.

I didn't know it then, but years later, when I'd need a different kind of sanctuary—one with soft lighting and couches instead of crates, one where I could sit and breathe instead of dance until I disappeared—I'd remember this moment.

The Hernandez family is planting seeds in the ruins of my old life.

Building something I didn't know I'd need.

* * *

Around that time, I started making trips up to Orlando, where the rave scene was still thriving. The city had its own pulse—brighter, younger, softer somehow. It was a place that still believed in the joy of it all.

At Firestone, the music never stopped. A warehouse full of lasers, fog, and kids who hadn't yet learned fear. They danced until sunrise, free and unbroken. It reminded me of why I fell in love with the music in the first place—before the headlines, before the paranoia, before the raids.

But no matter how far I went, Miami still had its hold.

One of the best DJs from Miami, as I recall vividly, was Rick Mitchell. As Kitty had advised me, Rick was a television engineer who had a knack for producing great things.

His cassettes were the best. My favorite was a Dorothy and Wizard of Oz mix from start to finish, mix/mixing in the hottest tracks of the day.

I was invited one weekend to go to Key West with Rick to help him promote his club night on a Saturday. It was my first and only trip that far south.

At the club, I heard a beat that I loved dancing to. "Free" by Ultra Naté began playing, and I jumped up and leaped onto the stage, only to be met with a performer coming out from behind the curtains, as this was their scheduled performance song. "Oops," I said, waving to the performer as I moved to one of the side boxes to continue dancing, much to the amazement of the scheduled performer.

* * *

Kitty invited me to her high-rise to drop something off. When I arrived, the apartment was full of drag queens from across the country—all in town preparing for an upcoming show.

I think it was for one of the pageants. They were about to preview the CD for the upcoming White Party.

True to South Beach fashion, Kitty played two songs from the CD that will be ingrained in my heart and soul and will play over and over in my mind forever. The first was "Together Again" by Janet Jackson, which was about to be released and told the story of loss many of us were going through at the time because of the AIDS epidemic.

The next was "Peace Train" by Dolly Parton, which was a fabulous take on the existential crisis that comes along with being a part of a lifestyle that is under attack by a vicious virus.

Dolly had been one of my favorites since I bought the first vinyl for my

Fisher-Price record player, with "Nine to Five" on one side and my all-time favorite, "Here You Come Again," on the other.

We all sat enjoying cocktails and reflecting on how blessed we were––first, to be friends with an icon, Kitty, who to this day does not get the recognition that they should, and second, knowing we were living in an age and time that would change the direction and course of our not-yet-termed LGBTQ+ history by fighting to stay alive and represent our true selves, which for those in the high-rise that night meant performance art and gender expressed through drag.

As the White Party was approaching, I met a group of promoters from New York who had arrived to host an event during the White Party weekend, one of Miami's biggest annual celebrations of music, art, and excess.

They were bringing their brand of New York spectacle down south—and they wanted authenticity, edge, *style*. Someone whispered my name.

Before long, my roommate Chastity and I were invited to host their party at a club called Zen, one of South Beach's hottest spots that season.

Hosting in Miami meant more than showing up—it meant embodying the fantasy. So we went all in: white vinyl, feathered accessories, and a touch of the supernatural. We turned heads the moment we walked in.

The night was a blur of lights and flashes—photographers circling, DJs spinning deep tribal tracks, bodies moving like liquid silver. Chastity and I weren't just hosts; we were part of the atmosphere itself. People came to Zen that night *because* of us—to see what we'd wear, to watch how we moved, to feel like they were part of the myth.

It was my first taste of being paid not just to attend the party, but to *be* the party.

The New York promoters were impressed—the way Ghost worked a room, the way Chastity balanced chaos with grace. "You two have to come to New York," they said. "We could use this kind of energy up there."

At the time, it sounded like flattery. I didn't realize it was foreshadowing.

I was also privileged to attend the main event as a guest of the hosts that year. When I arrived at the entrance, there stood Kitty and Paloma. Kitty looked like a knight in sequin armor, and Paloma looked like a princess or queen of the court. The outfits for the White Party are legends in and of themselves. The same crowd of circuit partygoers with matching extravagant outfits.

* * *

Previously, word had spread that Madonna was about to release a new album, and the anticipation was electric.

When her Miami release party was announced, it was the event everyone wanted to attend—every promoter, every performer, every celebrity. We plotted for weeks to make it inside. But in a twist only South Beach could deliver, most of the local nightlife elite were quietly told to stay away. They wanted to save the energy for when Madonna herself arrived a few weeks later for her private appearance. Still, the buzz was intoxicating.

Even the idea of Madonna showing up had the whole city shimmering.

For those of us who'd built our lives around performance, she was the ultimate validation—proof that art and identity could collide and still look beautiful.

This became my first trip to New York, and it came like a pulse—spontaneous, electric, impossible to refuse. Dallas and her partner were going, and they convinced me to come along. The timing was perfect.

It wasn't just an event. It was a cultural moment.

We packed light but dressed heavy—glitter, leather, attitude, and an unspoken hunger to *belong* among the legends.

When we landed, the city felt alive in a way Miami never could—cold, metallic, and sharp, like a spark waiting to catch. Inside The Roxy, light and sound collided until you couldn't tell which was which.

When Madonna appeared, the energy shifted—the air itself felt holy. *Ray of Light* wasn't just an album; it was a declaration that transformation was survival.

After the party, Dallas and I wandered through the city, half-frozen and euphoric. Somewhere between the steam grates and the neon, I realized New York wasn't another chapter—it was another dimension.

After the Roxy, those same New York promoters I'd worked with in Miami reappeared, this time on their home turf. "Come out with us tonight," they said. "We'll show you how we do it uptown."

They brought me to The Sound Factory, a nightclub built inside an old gymnasium--a temple of lights, lasers, and sweat. The walls still had echoes of its past—basketball hoops above strobe lights, bleachers turned into VIP platforms. It was surreal, like partying inside a hallucination of Americana gone disco.

They handed me a VIP wristband the moment I walked in.

"You're family now," one of them said.

That night, I met Jonathan Fuentes, the voice behind the fabulous track "Somebody Stole My Glasses", and DJ Jonathan Peters, two of the biggest names in the New York circuit scene. Peters' set was a revelation—deep, relentless, spiritual. The sound didn't just fill the room, it *possessed* it.

I danced until morning, surrounded by promoters, drag icons, and club legends who had once felt unreachable. Now I was among them.

It hit me somewhere between the bass drops: I had crossed over. Ghost wasn't just a Houston creation or a South Beach phenomenon anymore. He was becoming something bigger—a name whispered from coast to coast, a presence that moved between cities like smoke.

* * *

The plan had been to stay a few days, catch Madonna, and fly home. But New York had other plans.

I stayed—days folding into nights; nights stretching into something timeless. I met Spencer, a friend of Ted's and a master connector in the nightlife world. Spencer never stopped moving—three phones, two assistants, one endless network. He brought me into the machinery—promotion, marketing, image management: the business of being unforgettable.

It was Spencer who took me to The Tunnel for the first time.

Walking into that club was like crossing a threshold into another universe. Massive, dark, hypnotic—strobes slicing through fog, lasers bouncing off walls, every inch vibrating with sound. It was everything the legends had promised. The Tunnel itself had six separate entrances. I entered through the furthest room. Each of these entrances had "tunnels" that emptied into the main dance floor. Lady Bunny would greet me and give me a long rope of drink tickets, saying, "Thanks for showing up for me back on the beach with Elaine."

There, I met some of the original club kids I'd grown up idolizing—Richie Rich, who had just released a cover of Olivia Newton John's classic "Magic," dressed as a unicorn. He was dressed as a floating genie that night at The Tunnel, shouting to get someone's--hell, everyone's--attention. Radiant and mischievous, Richie Rich ... expressing what I'd come to realize about the club kids: that we were artists, performers, living art. Downstairs in the lounge, I was able to sit next to and meet Lady Miss Kier--still divine, still dancing to "Groove Is in the Heart," the song that had shaped an era.

For the first time, I wasn't just a fan. I was a peer.

* * *

I'd become friends with Sapphire, a female DJ who worked with Spencer Productions. One night, it was cold and snowing—everything covered in white, sparkling, magical. We went to Twilo. Standing in line, Sapphire kept saying, "They're not gonna let me in. They're not gonna let me in."

When we got to the door, she was right. The doorman looked at her and said, "This is a gay club. You need to find somewhere else to go."

But I went in anyway.

Inside Twilo, Junior Vasquez was on the decks. The music was intense— deep, relentless, hypnotic.

That's when I ran into Kevin Aviance again—the same one who'd kicked me out of the Delano party in Miami. He ran up and gave me a huge hug.

"It's you!" he shouted over the music. "You're here with all the other club kids!"

I watched a model-style catwalk competition happen on the dance floor. Around 2 a.m., exhausted, we retreated to the lounge and collapsed onto inflatable 1970s-style chairs. We weren't sitting long when I heard it—that bumping sound that would become one of my favorite tracks: Razor and Guido's "Do It Again.: It was like the Pied Piper, drawing everyone back to the dance floor.

We obliged.

Dancing to that song, I thought: *The New York club scene has it all.*

* * *

Spencer had invited me to stay at Ted's penthouse apartment overlooking the Met Life building. While I was there, Ted showed up one day, ringing the doorbell with some bouncer-looking dude. I called Spencer, and he said ignore them, don't let them in, but they were banging on the door, so I did what any smart Ghost would do: I opened the door just enough to get out with it shutting behind me, and attempted to run down the hallway and out of the building. Ted grabbed me and asked what I was doing in HIS place. I wiggled my way out and past them. The add-on that Ted had with him wanted nothing to do with what was going on as I heard him saying, "I didn't sign up for this."

I made it to the stairs on the street, which was at Park Avenue and 5th, chose a building, entered and found an open office space to hide in. The people were nice--it was a literary office: once again, an ironic situation to describe years later back in Texas, given that I am writing this memoir. This was one of many times I avoided my demise by using the club kid rules.

In my attempt to establish myself in New York, I began promoting an upcoming circuit party being held at the Octagon nightclub. I was hanging out with Jude the son of a famous author of a scandalous Hollywood memoir, another crush on someone who I would never be with, since they were not gay. At some point, after the party was a flop and things in New York were looking dreadful, including the blizzard weather, Spencer was not happy that we were not actively promoting his events as he wanted and so Jude convinced me to board a Greyhound bus to Austin, where my friend Cody from Dallas was living. After a brief stay in Austin, I detoured to Victoria to visit my sister and niece before making my way to Houston and then Miami.

* * *

Eventually, I drifted south again, back to South Beach. By the time I returned, it was the end of season—that strange, time when the models fled north, and the city exhaled.

I ran into Ted one night. He looked me up and down and smirked.

"You should get a tattoo of the Ghostbusters guy—make it official."

I laughed. But I knew the rules.

Rule One: Always go by your club name.

Rule Two: No photos.

Rule Three: No tattoos.

And the sacred commandments from TJ and Anson:

Never look like you need to be there.

Never pay for your drugs.

Never go out before midnight.

Those were the codes we lived by. We thought they were keeping us safe, but really, they were keeping us bound to the illusion.

By then, Ghost wasn't just a character anymore—he was a legend in motion. I'd become part of a circuit that stretched from Houston to Miami to New York and back again. But with every new city, every new crowd, I felt myself fading a little more behind the mask.

The music was louder. The lights were brighter.
But the boy behind the makeup was starting to disappear.
Still, Ghost danced.
Because that's what Ghost did.

10

Behind The Ropes

On the best nights, the line outside the club looked less like people waiting and more like evidence that gravity worked differently here.

Bodies leaned, draped, and stacked along the sidewalk, pressed up against steel barricades and each other. Sequins flashed, and cigarette tips burned like tiny warning lights in the dark. Someone's perfume mixed with weed smoke, cheap cologne, and the sour breath of the city, all of it swirling together like a spell you had to walk through to get inside. The bass leaked out through the walls in slow, steady throbs, like the building itself had a heartbeat.

When I first arrived on the beach, I used to stand on the other side of that velvet rope at Liquid and wonder if I'd ever belong to a world like this. Now, I was part of the machinery that decided who got in.

The velvet rope was never just a rope. It was a border, a filter, a test. On one side: the hopefuls, the tourists, the kids who had seen some version of this life in a music video or a magazine and thought they were ready. On my side: the insiders, the regulars, the promoters, the door whores, the creatures of the night who understood the unspoken rules.

We were the velvet machinery/machine. And on most nights, I was proud to be a part of it.

One night, out of the blue, I was asked to work the door at Zen. One of the promoters had decided to secretly open the club for a Sunday morning after-hours. I thought it was a joke.

"Ghost, you're wasted back there in the dark," he said, waving his hand toward the dance floor. "I need you out front. You're a look. You're a vibe. You're a curation."

He stretched the last word out like it tasted expensive.

I had been going to the club long enough that the bartenders knew my drink, the bathroom attendants knew my secrets, and the DJ knew which tracks would drag me to the middle of the floor like a magnet. I came in on promoter lists, friend lists, special lists—names scrawled next to other names that didn't belong in daylight. I was part of the scenery, one of the familiar faces that blurred into the night's landscape.

"Curation?" I repeated, laughing.

He pointed at me. "Exactly. That laugh. That face. That energy. You're gonna stand at the rope and help me build the room before the room even starts."

I didn't know you could build a room that way, but I was about to learn. Working the door was theatre and triage.

From my spot at the velvet rope, I could see everything: the sidewalk performing its own show, the cab doors opening like stage curtains, the nervous hands smoothing down dresses or tugging at too-tight shirts, people checking their reflection in a car window and trying to decide who they were going to be tonight.

It wasn't about being pretty. That was the first lesson.

Pretty was everywhere. Pretty was cheap. What we were looking for was something else—an attitude, a risk, a story. Someone pretty who got dressed in the dark during an electrical storm and decided that was enough. Someone whose eyeliner said "I dare you," and whose shoes said "I don't care."

Sometimes the promoter would lean in close and mutter, "We're dying. Get me a crowd." Other nights, "Too many straight boys. Clean it up." Or, "We need freaks. Real ones. Not the Halloween kind."

And I'd start making decisions.

You.

Yes. You're boring, but your friend is interesting.

You two can come in if you leave him outside.

You, in the expensive dress and dead eyes.

Come back when you've lived a little.

You, with the split lip and glitter smeared across one cheek like a war mark? Go right in. Tell the DJ I sent you.

I didn't know it then, but all the things that had made me feel out of place in church, at Bible college, even at AstroWorld, were suddenly assets. My eye for the misfit, my hunger for the strange, my intuition about who was performing and who was surviving.

The line moved, stopped, shifted. The machine kept turning.

I also had the privilege of becoming friends with Gilbert from New York, often considered the master of the velvet rope and one of the original Palladium promoters and door people. He taught me that working the rope wasn't about power—it was about protection. Protecting the vibe, protecting the freaks, protecting the magic from those who would consume it without understanding it.

* * *

If Heaven in Houston had been my first glimpse of the promised land, this was something else entirely. Heaven had felt like stumbling into forbidden light; this was slotting into a system.

The club was more than just a building with loud music. It was a factory that turned loneliness into spectacle, pain into performance, trauma into a kind of twisted glamour. The bouncers, the bartenders, the dancers, the DJs, the promoters—we were all different parts of a body, working together without really understanding how. The money, the drugs, the looks, the lists, the backstage rooms and coat-check dramas—everything fed into the same machine.

And on some nights, it felt like the beach worshipped me.

"Ghost!" People shouted my name as they walked up, as if I controlled the whole operation. In those moments, with the rope hooked under my hand, I almost believed I did.

I thought about the boy in Waxahachie, sitting in the chapel, trying to pray away feelings he didn't have language for yet. I thought about the sixteen-year-old sneaking into Heaven with a fake ID and a heart that beat like a drumline. I thought about the kid who watched Madonna's *Truth or Dare* in a dark theater and felt something inside him finally say, *Yes, that. That's me.*

Now here I was, telling other lost kids yes or no at the gates.

I'd show up early, not in daylight—that was against the religion of nightlife—but early enough that the air still felt like possibility instead of sweat and regret. The staff would be smoking out front, trading last night's stories like baseball cards. Someone always owed someone else money. Someone was always owed an apology by someone else. No one ever actually settled.

Inside, the lights were up and unforgiving. The floors were sticky, the mirrors streaked with lipstick and last night's chaos. The club always looked smaller with houselights on—like a drag queen without her lashes. You could see every seam, every flaw, every trick the darkness had hidden.

We'd walk through it anyway, hands gesturing in the air as if we could already see the transformation: fog filling the corners, lasers slicing through the dark, bodies stacked against each other, the DJ lifting us and slamming us down like waves against a seawall.

"You'll be at the rope, obviously," the promoter would say, mapping out the night. "But after 2 a.m., I want you inside. Host mode. You're good at making lost boys feel found."

I shrugged, but the words lodged somewhere in me. Maybe that's what we all were. There were moments, though, when it all made sense.

A kid would walk up to the rope, shaking, clutching a fake ID like it was a passport to another planet. I recognized the fear instantly because it was mine, too, once. The way they stood a little too straight, like bracing for impact. The way their eyes darted, looking for danger and salvation at the same time.

I'd lean in, pretending to inspect the ID. "First time?" I'd ask softly.

Maybe they'd lie.

Maybe they'd confess.

Perhaps they'd nod, unable to say anything at all.

I'd step aside, lift the rope, and gesture toward the door. "Welcome home," I'd say, like a benediction.

Inside, the lights would swallow them. The music would rearrange their molecules. And I'd feel this strange mix of pride and guilt, like I'd just handed them both a key and a loaded gun.

One Sunday morning, about a dozen local celebrities and performers—including Kitty and Paloma—stayed until 9 or 10 a.m., lounging in the middle of the vacant dance floor, just chilling as a group of insiders. Being inside a club long after the doors had closed and the bars were shut down, the music barely audible in the background, was a moment of inclusion like no other.

They were still in full makeup, heels kicked off, laughing about nothing and everything. They weren't performing anymore. They were just ... being.

Paloma waved me over. "Sit down, Ghost. You're one of us now."

I sat.

The floor was interesting, a mix of armbands and lost attire. The lights made everyone look a bit worn (never tired). But sitting there in that circle—surrounded by legends who'd stopped pretending, who'd let me see behind the curtain—I felt something I hadn't felt in years.

I belonged.

* * *

Of course, the machine had a cost.

At first, it was little things. Sleep went first. Food went next. Honest conversations disappeared somewhere around my third espresso and fifth vodka. My phone filled up with numbers I never called in daylight. People told me secrets in bathrooms, and I forgot them as soon as we stepped out into the music, because there was always another song, another drama, another emergency.

Someone's ex showed up unexpectedly. Someone's dealer didn't. Someone's fantasy crashed into someone else's reality. Fights happened in gestures, in glares, in who got waved in and who got told, "Not tonight, babe."

The drugs helped and didn't help. They kept me upright when my body wanted to collapse, but they also loosened the edges of everything.

My sense of time, my sense of self, my sense of understanding. Ghost and the man underneath—both of them smudged together like lipstick on a collar.

Now and then, in the middle of the madness, I'd catch a glimpse of myself in a mirror behind the bar or a shiny wall panel. Not just the outfit or the eyeliner or the hair, but the eyes. They were hungry, not just for attention or beauty or drama, but for something I couldn't name.

The machine hummed louder.

We lost people to overdoses, to bad trips, to bad lovers, to their own shadows. Sometimes the machine chewed them up quietly, their absence explained away with a shrug and a "You know how it is." Sometimes the loss was loud, a memorial night when everyone cried and promised to take better care of each other.

We meant it.

For a while.

Then the lights went down, and the machine kept turning.

I told myself I was in control. That I could step away whenever I wanted. That this was just a phase, just another chapter. I'd done it before—left Bible college, left Houston, left Dallas, left versions of myself behind like old costumes.

But the truth is, the velvet machine had its fingers deeper in me than I wanted to admit.

Even my friends from Houston noticed. When Roxy came to visit, she got the full treatment—limos waiting at the airport when she mentioned my name, no cover charges, no waiting behind ropes.

"Everyone knows you," she said on her last night, watching yet another door open without us asking.

I didn't know how to explain that this was exactly what I'd been chasing. Not the limos or the free drinks. The recognition. The belonging. The proof that I mattered.

Years later, she'd tell me she could never go back to Miami. "It won't be the same," she said. "That magic doesn't exist anymore."

She was right. That version of South Beach—the one that opened its doors to anyone willing to transform themselves—is gone. What we had was unrepeatable.

And maybe that's what made it worth losing everything for.

* * *

Eventually, I tried my hand at promoting on South Beach. It did not go well.

Working to fill a nightclub with partygoers was one lesson in humility I won't easily forget.

* * *

Eventually, I tried my hand at promoting on South Beach. It did not go well. It was a lesson in humility I won't easily forget.

I had secured a Friday night "test" launch party at Salvation, which, up to that point, was mainly known for its Saturday nights. At first, I asked DJ Bugie—the same one who'd rejected my CD at Paloma's birthday party—to spin, but Bugie had a recurring position on Fridays at Twist. He was the one who recommended DJ David Mercado.

Everything was locked in: the date, the DJ, the 6 x 9 glossy fliers fresh from the printer. The Shop, a boutique on Washington Avenue, was sponsoring the night, even providing a station-wagon shuttle (the taxis in the '90s were '80s-style station wagons) to ferry people between the store and the club. This party wasn't just another party—this was an operation.

When I arrived at the club right at opening, it was vacant.

I remember Kitty and Paloma coming out to show support, but only about a dozen people showed up in total. The dance floor echoed. The DJ played to empty air. My grand launch was a ghost town. The dead party that never happened tarnished my reputation and ended my South Beach promoter career before it began.

For years after, I carried a box full of thousands of leftover fliers—a physical reminder of my failure. They would have been more useful distributed among stores before the event, rather than sitting in that box as a monument to my hubris. I learned a hard truth that night: working the rope and being the promoter were two very different skills.

One required intuition and presence

The other hustle needed a strategy and a network I didn't yet have. I would use this lesson back in Houston years later and, for a time, become a somewhat successful promoter.

But that night in Miami, standing in an empty Salvation with Kitty's sympathetic eyes on me, I understood something important:

The machine gave me power at the rope.

But it didn't provide me with everything.

* * *

The machine had its own gravity. And sometimes, it pulled in planets.

One night, a black SUV rolled up and out stepped the stars of the upcoming film "Something about Mary" *Yes, it's really us, please pretend it isn't.*

The line stalled. People whispered.

But when they reached me, they looked ... unsure.

Not starstruck--unsure.

Human unsure.

The same way the eighteen-year-old baby gays looked when they held out their fake IDs with trembling hands.

"Hey," the actress said, with a grin that could melt headlines. "So … do we go in this way?"

I smiled. "Everybody goes in this way."

The Lead Actor on the film laughed—a nervous laugh, the kind you recognize instantly when you've spent years around people who build personas for a living.

They weren't there to be celebrities.

They were there to disappear.

The actress lowered her voice. "We heard this place is wild."

"It can be," I said. "Depends on the crowd."

That's when she did it—the thing that made me understand the moment we were in.

She looked past me.

Past the rope.

Past the bouncers.

At our freaks.

Our creatures.

Our misfits.

Our drag angels.

Our beautiful, broken, brilliant monsters.

"This," she whispered, "is the real Hollywood."

I don't think she meant it as a compliment.

I think she meant it as the truth.

I lifted the rope.

"Welcome to Groove," I said.

They stepped inside, swallowed by the darkness, by the world that built me. And standing there with the rope in my hand, I had a realization so sharp it cracked something open inside me:

For the first time, I wasn't looking at fame.

Fame was looking at us.

At me.

At the subculture that raised me.

At the machine I helped run.

It wasn't celebrity meets nightclub.

It was celebrity meets subculture—and subculture won.

Years later, I'd watch *There's Something About Mary*—the movie they were filming in Miami during that time—and recognize our South Beach in the background, captured on Hollywood film. Our freaks. Our streets. Our world turned into a backdrop for their story. They took our electricity and sold it back to the world.

But that night, they were just two people trying to touch something real.

And we were it.

* * *

Some nights, after the last person stumbled out and the lights came up harsh and unforgiving, I'd walk back through the space slowly. The fog would be thinning, the floor a graveyard of broken heels, lost earrings, and smeared fliers. The DJ would be coiling cords, the bartenders counting tips, the bouncers finally letting their shoulders drop.

I'd stand in the middle of the dance floor, look up at the lights, and hear the echo of the night that had just happened—laughter, screams, the collective roar when a favorite song hit. The ghost of it all passing through me.

Ghost. The name I'd chosen. The name the machine had learned to say.

In those moments, I understood why people called nightlife a religion. We came together, we transformed, we sacrificed, we confessed. We worshipped the beat, the light, each other. We left exhausted and emptied, promising ourselves we'd be better, cleaner, calmer—right up until the following invitation, the next flier, the next theme night pulled us back in.

The velvet machine was hungry.

So was I.

From the Regency to the Commodore, from Salvation to Liquid, I had become part of the rhythm—a cog in the velvet machine of South Beach nightlife.

People were saying my name in conversations. The people who worked the doors of other clubs welcomed me with open ropes. But even in the spotlight, I could feel something humming beneath the surface—a faint static of disconnection. A sense that the machine I'd helped feed was starting to feed on me.

The nights were dazzling, the faces flawless, but I knew—deep down—that even the brightest lights eventually burn out.

For now, though, I danced.

For now, Ghost still glittered.

11

Last Season

By 1998, South Beach had become a mythology—and somehow, I was one of its ghosts made flesh.

My name was on the lips of promoters, whispered through dressing rooms, printed on party fliers in silver ink. Ghost had become part of the city's vocabulary.

But behind the glitter and the flashbulbs, Miami was changing. The clubs were still loud, still luminous, but the light was shifting—harsher, colder, thinner at the edges.

It was the last season before everything fell apart.

Miami was alive, or maybe it was just refusing to die. Either way, I was still in the middle of it all, chasing the same high that had brought me here in the first place.

South Beach was changing. The music was harder, the nights longer, but the air felt heavier—charged with something uneasy. After Versace's murder, the city had never been the same. The glamour was still there, but a shadow had joined it.

You could see it in the streets: the FBI, DEA, and local law enforcement swarming the beach. The old guard had been swept out and replaced by outsiders—agents flown in to get control of a nightlife that had become international news. They carried thick binders labeled "JTF"—Joint Task Force—walking down Collins Avenue like soldiers patrolling an occupied city.

For those of us who had lived the scene from the inside, it was surreal.

Still, we tried to hold on. The party always finds a way.

* * *

The late-night sanctuaries—the after-hours clubs that had defined Miami's heartbeat—began to fall one by one.

There was Hombres, dark and sweaty, tucked away from the tourist traps. It was the kind of place that came alive after 4 a.m., when everything else had gone silent. There, people moved like shadows—drag queens, dancers, hustlers, lovers—all chasing that last spark before sunrise.

Then came Equis, a short-lived experiment in decadence. By day, it was a restaurant; by night, it became an underground after-hours spot. But the magic couldn't last. Within weeks, it was raided and shut down.

CHROME followed—a sleek, industrial space that had once promised to revive the energy of the old scene. It burned bright for a few seasons, full of smoke, strobes, and sweat. But even that light dimmed when the raids began to spread north.

I met one of the founders during this time. He explained that CHROME was an acronym, though I can't remember what it stood for today. The club is located in an unsuspecting shopping center with doctors' offices and retail, on Lincoln Drive, one of Miami Beach's main shopping destinations. I remember walking past the construction where they were building the new theater using the facade of an art deco building.

I went to CHROME a couple of times before the city, under advisement from national law enforcement, shuttered its doors—another victim of the Joint Task Force and anti-rave laws that were tearing apart the after-hours scene and my life on South Beach.

And then came The Mix, hosted by David Padilla, one of Miami's most beloved DJs. Padilla's sets could resurrect the dead—deep, soulful, hypnotic: the kind of music that made you forget how close the sun was.

The Mix became the city's oxygen after dark, one of the last true safe havens for those of us still living the nightlife dream. But even that was temporary. The anti-rave ordinances hit hard in the late '90s, banning all-night events and cracking down on electronic music culture. The city wanted control, and the easiest way to find it was to turn off the music.

One by one, the lights went out.

* * *

I continued to move in and out of the circles I had become a part of——attending parties, seeking fashion adventures, and socializing here and there.

One of the funniest moments of my time in South Beach was when the drag queens needed to move.

Carlos, one of the circuit boys who often performed and was close with Kitty and Paloma, was recruited to help move the queens of the beach. You see, Kitty had secured a small house in upper Dade County, and Paloma was ready to grow out of her one-bedroom in central South Beach. So they devised a plan to coordinate a single swift move: Kitty out, Paloma in. One catch: it all had to be moved in one weekend.

So when I showed up to help move boxes, I found out that the U-Haul was ready for pickup at the rental location a few blocks away from Kitty's on the bay side of South Beach. Only catch: no one knew how to drive a stick shift.

However, having grown up in rural Texas, I knew not only how to drive a standard, but also had experience moving many times from Dallas to Houston and back. Carlos—one of Paloma's good friends—and I were "volunteered" to drive the U-Haul and do the heavy lifting.

I walked with Carlos to the storage facility, got the keys, and drove to Kitty's high-rise. We loaded boxes full of boas and sequin gowns—one of the most famous circuit drag icons moving from bay side to beach side.

Afterward, we went to load up Paloma and move one of Versace's early muses, and early recipient of breast implants, Paloma, from Central Beach to bay side, all the time leaving a trail of feathers along the way.

For three long, ridiculous days, we carted drag history across Miami. Wigs, boas, boxes of costumes, endless shoes, and makeup cases—all flying through the air as we turned corners. Kitty yelled directions from the passenger seat in full face and heels, Paloma shrieked about her wigs from the back, and José just laughed the whole time.

By the end of the move, Miami had officially seen the most fabulous moving truck in history—a caravan of glitter, chaos, and laughter barreling down Collins Avenue.

Even now, I can still picture it: the heat shimmering off the road, the U-Haul packed with tulle and tiaras, and the two reigning queens of South Beach swapping lives one box at a time.

The theme for this weekend was "No More Moving for Local Legends." A punchline and gag that we would carry through the end of that season. As a reward for all the hard work, Carlos threw an after-movement party where the Special K flowed.

One thing about Special K: it's a third-eye substance that can create some of the most *Twilight Zone* moments. Special K−−ketamine or esketamine−−was a party substance that was part of the trail mix those days.

A 10ml vial: pop the top, place in a Pyrex plate, and place on top of boiling water. This causes the clear liquid to crystallize into a powder. Add a few drops of vanilla and throw it in the freezer, and you have Vanilla Ice Ice Baby K. I can remember entering into a three-hour K-hole and having full-on discussions with everyone in that room, even though no words were ever uttered.

Hours later, as we left, we all agreed that we had had insightful conversations, without speaking at all the entire evening.

* * *

Unless you've lived there and experienced it, it's hard to understand that life in South Beach is very insular.

All the shops there are boutiques––individuals run most, and there's a different shop for everything. So, as you can imagine, when I loaded up Paloma and Kitty, we went to Walmart. It was a bit of a shock.

I remember that because both Paloma and Kitty were out of drag, some of the employees were staring at us. We definitely seemed out of place. As a kid, going to Kmart and Walmart was a regular thing, and it was quite familiar to me.

This time, it was different, since among the elements of the beach we somewhat stood out. We didn't get to spend much time in the store because too many people were gawking. Around every corner, someone was whispering about who the fags were that had invaded their store.

Paloma did not flinch. In and out of drag, she was the vision of beauty, appearing like Jessica Rabbit had stepped out of the screen, with, as I have mentioned, Double D breast implants that filled out every designer gown she put on. Walking down Ocean Drive Collins, or Washington, often brought catcalls, some kind, some not; either way, this diva with the thick accent would respond with a fierce knowledge that she had the world in her palms.

Kitty had been freelancing for the owners of the local fashion house who were planning a big show featuring Raymond Drago, a New York designer with a leather aesthetic who was gaining popularity and set to make his SOBE premiere.

In the week leading up to the event, I remember Kitty being stressed out by the demands of working for the German high-society owners, who had a mansion on Star Island, home to the rich and fabulous of Miami, including Rosie O'Donnell and Gloria Estefan.

I did everything I could to help make the show a success. In one of the funniest moments of my time on the beach, I remember being in front of Equis (the restaurant by day and nightclub by night) when the after-party from the fashion show was over. Leaving in a group were Kitty, the owners, Raymond and Little J, all looking frantic at the attention from the paparazzi as they loaded into the waiting ride. Inside, Kitty was worn out and relieved it was over, thankful to me for the help I had provided during the hectic weeks leading up to the show.

I had been in South Beach for months by the time I finally made my way to Lucky Cheng's. Little did I know that the likes of Chyna Girl, Connie Casserole, and others worked in drag at the world-famous drag cafe on Lincoln Avenue. Sherman Hemsley from *The Jeffersons* was there with tourists and locals alike. The drag performers served as your waiters and entertainers while you dined. The dressing room was full of a dozen or so of South Beach's most famous.

One by one, they came out on stage and performed drag classics. 'I remember being in the dressing room when Chyna Girl realized it was her turn on stage. She streaked some fresh lipstick across her face and ran out in heels, already lip-syncing the words to "I Will Survive" before she'd even hit the spotlight.

Connie looked up from her mirror and out the swinging door's small circular window, watching Chyna tear past.

"Chyna's always at her best when running behind schedule," she said with a knowing smile.

That was the magic of Lucky Cheng's—organized mayhem wrapped in sequins, where the queens turned lateness into performance art and every entrance was an event.

* * *

At the season's end, I got swept into several last moments of magic. First, my friend Paul Lynch of Lynchmob Productions was moving away, to LA, and I was fortunate to attend a farewell event at Glam Slam, the club owned by Prince himself.

That night felt untouchable—the heat, the lights, the electricity of a crowd that knew the end was near. Everyone who mattered showed up: queens, promoters, DJs, dancers, legends. The air vibrated with nostalgia and adrenaline.

And then, as if the night needed to seal itself in myth, Prince appeared. Just for a moment—silent, watching, impossibly cool—before slipping back into the darkness.

I remember standing there, drenched in sweat and glitter, thinking, *This is it. This is the dream.*

Legend has it that there was once a party at Glam Slam named Paragon where, due to the laws of the time, the person working the ropes would lock the door at precisely 2 a.m. sharp. Word has it that queens could be seen running up Collins Avenue to make it inside for a party that would go on well into the morning. Although I did not get to partake in this legendary party, I was privy to several Glam Slam moments while in South Beach.

Just after the farewell party for Paul Lynch, the doors to Glam Slam were quiet on a Friday night. I remember seeing Kitty and Nathan Judd at the late-night cafe on Collins, both very quiet and uncommunicative. A few weeks later, a full-page ad with the picture of Earth on it merely stated "World" coming soon. And just like that, Nathan owned the weekends from Friday at the World to Saturday Salvation.

Not every night was wild or tragic—some were just surreal, the kind of memories that stay sparkling in your mind forever.

One evening, Kitty, one of her friends who was a local fashion editor, and I decided to walk from the bay side to the ocean side of South Beach. It was one of those perfect Miami nights—the air thick with salt, the streets humming with possibility, and every block lit up like a movie set. Kitty was in heels, of course, gliding down the sidewalks like a queen holding court, and I trailed beside her, taking in the sights that felt almost too alive to be real.

As we crossed Washington Avenue, we suddenly heard a roar—cheering, screaming, fireworks bursting near downtown MiamiCentral. For a second, we thought we'd accidentally stumbled into one of those spontaneous street parades that seemed to erupt out of nowhere in South Beach. People were honking, shouting, waving flags, and confetti floated through the air as we walked into a dream.

We passed a convertible with fans leaning out, waving and shouting that the Florida Marlins had just won the World Series. It was pandemonium—joy spilling into the streets, strangers hugging, cars honking in rhythm. Kitty laughed and raised her arms like she was accepting an award, basking in the noise and light.

By the time we reached our destination—The Shop, the boutique on Washington—we were swept up in it too. It didn't matter that we hadn't planned to celebrate anything; in South Beach, life had a way of making you part of the show whether you meant to or not.

* * *

A week later, in a surprise turn of events, I found myself standing in the courtyard of the Delano Hotel under the warm buzz of champagne and victory. The city was still buzzing from the win. Somehow, in true South Beach fashion, I found myself hosting the unofficial private World Series after-party at Lucky 13, the hidden bar inside the Delano Hotel, one of the city's most exclusive lounges.

The players, their wives, models, and celebrities all swirled together under the same humid Miami night. Someone handed me a flute of champagne, and I remember thinking, *I've made it. I'm standing in the center of everything I used to dream about.*

It wasn't about money or fame—it was about belonging to a moment so alive it refused to end. But nothing in nightlife lasts forever. It felt like the universe had turned the volume up again—champagne everywhere, flashes from cameras, music pulsing through the white marble halls.

The Marlins players and their wives came in still glowing from victory, all charm and disbelief, as if none of it had quite sunk in yet.

The night blurred into laughter, dancing, and toasts that went long past dawn. Between the velvet ropes and the cigarette smoke, I remember thinking how strange it was—just a week before, I'd been walking through confetti as a spectator. Now, I was standing behind the bar with the champions, a part of the story instead of someone watching from the street.

In those moments, South Beach didn't just feel alive—it felt enchanted.

But for every peak, there's a comedown.

And for Ghost—for me—that fall was already written.

* * *

After Glam Slam and the Mix, Gary James—the eternal reinventor—opened a new venue: The Shadow Lounge.

It was everything the name promised: dark, sleek, dangerous, and glamorous in that uniquely Miami way, located in a former church, with all of the glory of the Limelight in New York but with a South Beach twist. The DJ booth was elevated in the middle of the dance floor, beaming down through glass, looking more like an alien spaceship than a DJ Booth. In the restroom on the ladies' side, there was a two-way mirror that allowed those on that side to see what the guys were up to.

One night, Gary teased a planned future special event—Ghost and Daisy Deadpetals hosting side by side.

Still a prominent figure in South Beach to this day, back then Daisy was a young up and coming drag performer regarded highly by the south beach elte and one of the nicest people I would meet during my time on the beach. That night, I felt like everything had come full circle. From Houston to South Beach, from the dance floor to the spotlight—I was no longer just part of the scene. I *was* the scene. But beneath the champagne smiles and camera flashes, I could feel it—the shift. The crowd was thinning, the energy different. The old faces were disappearing, replaced by new ones who didn't know what the scene had once been.

Miami was changing. The world was changing.

And I could feel Ghost fading.

* * *

That final season in South Beach was the end of an era—the last dance before the lights came up. The parties were still wild, the names still glittered, but something essential had slipped away.

I remember one of those last nights vividly. Kitty was hosting. Paloma was in full regalia, her gown her gown dancing in the light. I wore silver from head to toe—a reflection of everything we once were.

The music was pure nostalgia—old-school anthems that had built the scene. When CeCe Peniston's "Finally" came on, the crowd erupted like it was 1991 all over again.

For a moment, it really was. But when the lights came up, I felt something I hadn't before—a deep, aching stillness.

The party was over.

Ghost wasn't a mask anymore.

He was an equation—a balance of art, rebellion, and danger.

I'd learned from the best: from Houston's anarchists, Dallas's drag queens, and Miami's golden idols. I didn't want to live the scene—I wanted to embody it. To show that beauty and chaos could coexist, that glamour could have grit, that a boy from Texas could build a legend out of smoke, mirrors, and music. I was chasing something no drug could give me: immortality in memory. But in Miami, where everyone came to be seen, I was about to learn that sometimes the spotlight burns hotter than anyone can survive.

Soon after, I packed up my apartment off Washington and 14th, said my goodbyes to Dallas, Chyna Girl, and Chastity, and took one last slow walk down Ocean Drive.

The palm trees swayed in the salt-heavy air. Neon signs buzzed above shuttered storefronts. The ghosts of laughter and bass echoed faintly between the buildings.

It was beautiful—and hollow.

The flight back to Houston wasn't planned, but it felt inevitable. My suitcase was half-full of clothes, half-full of memories—club fliers, Polaroids, glitter-stained fabric, and a few empty vitamin bottles I should've left behind.

As the plane lifted off, I watched the lights of Miami shrink into a jeweled blur below—pink, gold, electric, fading.

The city that had built me, broken me, and baptized me in neon was finally slipping away. For the first time in years, there was silence. No bass, no chatter, no laughter spilling out of open doors. Just the low hum of the engines and the sound of my own heartbeat. I told myself I was going home, that Houston would be different—that I could finally rest.

But as the clouds swallowed the skyline, I had the strangest feeling:

The story wasn't finished.

Something was still chasing me.

Something unseen, patient, waiting for me to land.

I closed my eyes and whispered, "Goodbye, Ghost."

But deep down, I knew he wasn't gone.

He was only changing form.

IV

Fall

South Beach, 1998. The scene that made Ghost a legend was about to destroy him. As the Joint Task Force closed in and club after club fell to raids, the glittering world of velvet ropes and VIP rooms revealed its darker side. When the music finally stopped and the lights came up for the last time, Ghost had a choice: stay and face the consequences or run home to rebuild. But some falls you can't stop—you can only survive the landing.

12

Ghostbusters

Back in Houston, life felt quieter—but underneath the calm, something buzzed. It started small: random phone calls, wrong numbers that weren't really wrong, people dropping my name in conversations I hadn't been part of.

It was not long after my return that I had settled into an efficiency apartment in the Westmoreland district of Montrose.

I was living in the same complex as my girlfriend, Tori, and Emily, who was dating the door guy from SOME, who had always had a particular disdain for me.

Herald was the door guy I had watched carry one of the most muscular guys I had ever laid eyes on out the door from the men's restroom past The feminine-leaning club kid named Walpaper in the girls' room, as usual, through the dance floor, and out the emergency exit.

Due to my association with Tori and Emily, instead of making me wait in line, which he knew I abhorred, Harold greeted me with a nicer resolve at the door. But it didn't last long, since a few weeks after my return, the owners put out fliers that club SOME was closing its doors for good.

They had a weekend of events, and I remember running into my old bartender Andy, who was a shadow of his former self. The old network was shifting. Same faces, same patterns, but this time everything felt ... watched.

That's when Bob, one of Ted's close associates, resurfaced.

He had that same knowing smile, the kind that said too much without words. We met a few times around Montrose—exchanged a few things, shared a few laughs—but the air was heavier now.

The world that had once felt glamorous now felt as if it were holding its breath. It didn't last long. Maybe a couple of months, at most. Then came that morning. Then there was Bubba—a wiry, fast-talking character I'd met in Monroe, Louisiana. At first, he seemed harmless, another transient face in a string of party acquaintances. But before long, he started traveling—north to Pittsburgh, east to meet people he shouldn't have been meeting—and eventually straight to Ted.

That was when everything began to crack.

Bubba had gone over my head, aligning himself with Ted and others who were already drawing attention from the wrong kind of people. Whether he was careless or calculated didn't matter—the damage was done. Around the same time, Jim, José's old roommate—a muscle-bound jock with an easy smile and a body built for attention—started hanging around more. He and Ted were inseparable, traveling together and, half-jokingly, wearing DEA and FBI shirts like they were costumes.

But nothing about that was funny.

After Versace's death, South Beach had been swarming with outsiders— federal agents, narcotics units, and a Joint Task Force presence that had crept across state lines. Houston wasn't immune. The same clean-cut men with government-issue haircuts had infiltrated Houston, cruising Main Street and downtown near the Spy Club, watching from unmarked cars.

Ted started warning everyone:

"Stop using the damn phones."

Cell phones were still new, heavy, unreliable, but dangerously traceable.

He wasn't wrong.

One afternoon, I opened my PrimeCo bill and nearly dropped it. Over $2,500 in charges—every call, every minute, every contact, logged in black and white. It wasn't just a bill; it was a map of my movements, a confession printed on paper.

The laughter faded after that. Conversations grew shorter. People stopped using names, stopped showing up where they used to. Even the clubs felt strange—too bright, too open, too full of ghosts waiting to see who would fall next.

* * *

Looking back, I must have known something was coming.

The air had changed in ways I couldn't name—phone calls that ended when I walked into rooms, cars that lingered too long outside my building, the feeling of being watched even when I was alone.

The Ghost who'd once moved through Houston's nightlife, invisible, now felt exposed, transparent, as if everyone could see through the costume to the person underneath, who was breaking apart.

So I did what I always did when the world felt too close: I threw one last party.

Through Tori, I'd met Secret—an exotic dancer with a safe full of party supplies and a laugh that could light up a room. She had connections everywhere–the kind of friend who could make anything happen with a phone call and a smile. When I told her I needed one more night—one perfect, electric, unforgettable night—she didn't ask why. She just made it happen.

The crew gathered at my apartment that evening: the Houston regulars, the late-night believers, the ones who'd been there through the chaos and hadn't walked away yet. Secret arrived with news that made everyone scream— she'd secured a limo for the night. And not just any limo. A stretched white limousine with neon lights inside and a driver who didn't ask questions.

"We're doing this right," she said, grinning. "One club? No. We're hitting them all."

The first stop was Rich's—the place where Ghost had first appeared years ago, where everything had started. Walking through those doors felt like stepping into a memory I was already mourning. The music hit differently that night. Every beat felt urgent, every light felt brighter, every face felt like goodbye.

From Rich's, we rolled to SOME—the eternal after-hours. Then downtown to the smaller haunts, the backroom bars, the after-hours spots where the authentic Houston lived.

Secret was electric all night—dancing on tables, pulling strangers into our orbit, making the limo feel like a spaceship traveling through the city's veins. At some point, the line between performance and reality dissolved. The laughter got louder. The touches lingered longer.

By the time we made it back to my apartment—just the two of us, the rest of the crew dropped off at various corners of the city—the sun was threatening the horizon. We stumbled inside, still buzzing, still riding the high of a night that had felt like defiance.

And then it happened.

Not planned. Not expected. Just two people who'd spent the night running from something neither of us wanted to name, finding comfort in the only language we had left.

Afterward, lying there in the pre-dawn quiet, Secret traced patterns on my chest and said softly, "You know this can't last, right?"

I didn't answer.

Because I knew.

I'd been flying back and forth to South Beach for months—Houston to Miami, Miami to Houston, living two lives in two cities until neither felt real.

After my trip to New York, I drove through Austin to my oldest sister's house in Bay City. I picked up my 1990 Nissan Sentra—the exact car I'd bought working nights at Denny's, the same vehicle that had carried me to Powertools for the first time, to Rich's, to SOME, to every club that had ever mattered.

I'd left it in long-term parking at Intercontinental Airport before my last season in South Beach. When I returned—a month later, maybe more; time blurred in those days—I was surprised to find it still there, buried in the back of the storage lot like a relic I'd forgotten I owned.

I'd lost the parking ticket somewhere between Miami and reality. The attendant shrugged. "No ticket? Two-week minimum."

I paid it. Got someone to jump-start the engine. And drove out of that airport for what I didn't know then would be the last time.

The car smelled like stale air and old dreams. The passenger seat still had glitter ground into the fabric. A pair of sunglasses I didn't remember losing sat in the cupholder.

It felt like driving someone else's life.

* * *

Then the knock came.

I was still half-asleep, Secret already gone, the apartment smelling like smoke and yesterday's freedom. When I opened the door, my parents stood there—my dad holding a folded piece of paper, his face carved in stone.

He didn't say a word. Just handed it to me.

The note was anonymous, written in a rushed scrawl:

"Your son's apartment is going to be raided today. Get him out."

My heart dropped.

Everything slowed down, the way it does when the lights come on after the best night of your life, and you realize the music has already stopped.

My mother's eyes were red. My father looked older than I'd ever seen him.

"Pack," he said. "Now."

We didn't wait around to see if it was true. I grabbed what I could—clothes, a few photos, fragments of the life I'd built in this apartment, in this city, in this skin I'd worn for so long. The Ghost costume stayed behind. The platform shoes. The fliers with my name in bold letters.

I left it all.

We drove in silence—my dad gripping the wheel, my mother staring out the window, me in the backseat watching Houston disappear in the rearview mirror.

By the time we reached Louisiana, it was already in motion.

Whispers. Sealed papers. The words "indictment" and "investigation" passed across desks, handled by people who'd never stepped inside a nightclub, who'd never understood what we were building, who saw only crime where we'd seen community.

The knock at the door hadn't been a warning.

It had been an ending.

Weeks later--after the warning, after my parents arrived at my door with stone faces and an anonymous note--we went to the apartment together. My mother cried quietly while my father moved with grim efficiency, packing boxes in silence.

We boxed everything: the boas shedding feathers like old prayers, the platforms that had made me taller than I ever was, the face paint cracked and dried, the costumes that had once felt like armor and now looked like evidence.

"Save it for another day," my mother said, though neither of us believed there would be one.

I loaded it all into the Nissan—the car I'd bought with honest money, back when I thought freedom meant driving wherever I wanted, back when I didn't know the night could take more than it gave.

And then I drove east. Away from Montrose, away from the clubs, away from the lights and the bass and the version of myself I'd spent a decade building and a single morning dismantling. The Nissan carried me into exile the same way it had taken me into the night all those years ago.

Full circle.

Except now, the only thing glittering in the rearview mirror was Houston disappearing behind me.

* * *

It was during this time that I was stuck on my parents' couch, not at all ungrateful–it was much better than a prison bed.

The first few nights, I was going through severe withdrawals, hearing voices, sweating late at night, and feeling like I was being chased, only this time it wasn't real, like it was in Miami and New York.

I was able to take some time to gather my thoughts. I also spent some time at the church I grew up in, helping with chores and organizing. I was detoxing and looking for employment while we took several trips to New Orleans for pretrial proceedings.

During one of these meetings with my court-appointed attorney, she said that my name, Mark, had not come up during the investigation except once; however, they were still trying to figure out who this Ghost character was because he appeared in almost all the records. The club kid rules had saved me in more ways than one after all.

In the end, I would never testify to anything, because I really knew nothing. I merely had inadvertently been in the wrong place at the wrong time on occasion, and when it was over, I stood before the court—a far cry from the spotlight I'd once enjoyed.

In the end, I signed for six months' house arrest, six months' probation, and six months in a halfway house. A year and a half to rebuild a life I'd spent a decade tearing apart.

The silence that followed was deafening. No music. No lights. No Ghost. For the first time, it was just me … learning how to exist without the mask, and realizing that the real haunting had only just begun.

During probation, I tried to rebuild.

I worked small jobs, stayed out of trouble, and avoided the old haunts.

But the temptation to drift back into the scene was constant—that hum beneath the skin that never really goes away. I still ran into familiar faces around Houston—DJs, promoters, kids from the old days—some thriving, some broken, some pretending everything was fine.

It was strange to see the world keep spinning without me, to watch nightlife evolve while I stood still. The half-truths and ghosts of the past still lingered, but I was learning to breathe again. For the first time, Ghost was silent—but Mark was learning to live.

Houston felt different.

Not the heat—that was the same oppressive blanket it had always been.

Not the skyline—that still glittered at night like broken promises. What felt different was me.

I was no longer Ghost.

The plea bargain was simple on paper. But paper doesn't prepare you for the sound of your own name—your real name—spoken by a judge who doesn't care about platform shoes or spiral face paint or the fact that you once made rooms pulse just by walking through them.

I was Mark again.

And for the first time in years, that name felt like wearing someone else's skin.

13

Lockdown

The halfway house was a different kind of education.

Raw. Loud. Real.

A collection of men trying to rebuild from rubble, each with a story, each with a shadow. You learn a lot about people when everything you own fits in a duffel bag.

Mine contained the requisite three T-shirts—blue, as specified in the intake paperwork. Two khaki pants. Three pairs of white boxer briefs. Six pairs of socks. My two work shirts were already wrinkled—toiletries: one toothbrush, toothpaste, a brush, hair gel.

That was it.

Everything else—the platform shoes, the makeup, the costumes, the life I'd built in sequins and smoke—had been left behind in a cardboard box in a closet somewhere, gathering dust like evidence of a crime I was still paying for.

At intake, they handed me one roll of toilet paper and a locker key.

One roll.

As if to say: ration everything now—even dignity.

The indictment and subsequent charges were my first real time being in trouble—real trouble. This kind came with processing, orientation, and a two-person cubicle in a dorm that smelled like industrial cleaner and regret. The Cornell Facility sat on Commerce Street in downtown Houston, blocks from the first rave I'd ever attended, the same street where underground after-hours had once pulled me into the night like gravity.

I was a resident of a facility that was within walking distance of the places that had destroyed me.

Everyone there was fighting their own ghosts.

During the time I was at the halfway house, there was a curfew, but we were allowed to go into the parking lot or listen to music. The parking lot became our sanctuary—the only place we could be ourselves without supervision. Someone had a boom box. Someone else had burned CDs.

That's when I first heard Cher's "Believe."

Not just the song—the entire album. I played it until the CD scratched. "Life after love?" she asked through distorted speakers, her voice bouncing off concrete and metal gates.

I did. Or at least I was trying to.

Every night, I'd stand in that parking lot, listening to Cher ask the question I couldn't answer yet. I could sing that album front to back even now—every word a prayer I didn't know I was praying.

The halfway house just happened to be across the street from the new downtown baseball park, Minute Maid Park. I can remember watching the Enron Field being erected beam by beam and panel by panel as Houston's first downtown premier sports venue was being built right in front of my eyes. It was being built while I was being dismantled. Both of us were under construction. Both of us were trying to become something new.

The structure of leadership at Cornell Corrections was, to put it mildly, questionable. Gossip rippled through the facility like contraband—whispered in the mess hall, muttered during smoke breaks. The facility director had allegedly paid someone off and gained her position through nepotism, related to the owner by blood or favors——no one was quite sure which. Either way, the workers made their disdain clear in the way they said her name, clipped and cold, like spitting out something bitter.

That didn't last long.

* * *

Halfway through my stay, rumblings of a shakeup started—drama, even in lockup. Turned out the assistant director had played a role in the warden's termination—something about money laundering, fraud, the kind of charges that made the evening news. The details were fuzzy, but the result was clear: new management, tighter ship, or at least the performance of one.

It was around then that, as part of my weekly chores, each inmate was assigned specific duties. My assignment was to serve on the cleanup crew for the front entrance and processing area.

I was mopping near intake one afternoon when I heard the metal door buzz open. A line of new arrivals shuffled in—duffel bags, downcast eyes, the universal posture of men who'd just traded freedom for supervision.

And then I saw him.

Dan.

I froze mid-mop, water pooling at my feet.

He looked the same, with the same cocky grin, same energy that refused to dim even under fluorescent lights and shame. We'd partied together back when I lived in southwest Houston, back when nights had no consequences and mornings were optional.

The newly appointed director—formerly the assistant director, now running intake herself "to make sure the intake personnel did not make any mistakes"—was processing the group with mechanical efficiency. Duffel bags opened. Belongings cataloged. Contraband seized.

Dan caught my eye and winked. Then, with the most casual motion in the world, he held up a bottle of baby oil.

"We shall see about that," he said, just loud enough for me to hear. I had to turn away to keep from laughing.

The oldest trick in the book—GHB hidden inside, clear liquid in a clear bottle, sitting in plain sight among his toiletries. If you didn't know what you were looking for, you'd never know. And judging by the way the director waved him through without a second glance, she didn't.

Dan had smuggled the party into the lockup. And somehow, I wasn't even surprised.

A week later, during cleaning duties in the main dorm, Dan found me.

"You look like you could use a break," he said, holding up a water bottle that definitely wasn't water.

I should have said no.

I'd been sober for months—mandated, monitored, measured. Every piss test is a small victory. Every clean day, a brick in the wall I was rebuilding. But God, I missed feeling good.

Just once, I told myself. To remember what it felt like to float instead of drown.

I took a capful.

Then another.

Within twenty minutes, the edges softened. The oppressive hum of the facility—the distant arguments, the weight of two hundred men breathing the same recycled air—all of it faded into a warm, familiar glow.

For the first time in months, I felt like myself again—the Ghost I'd buried under khaki pants and supervision.

I cleaned that dorm like I was conducting a symphony—every mop stroke precise, every corner attended to with the kind of focus that only comes from being slightly out of your mind and deeply, blissfully high.

That weekend, Dan smuggled in something else: a pirated DVD of a brand-new movie no one outside had seen yet.

* * *

We gathered in the VIP dorm, the quieter wing reserved for those nearing release––fifty guys instead of two hundred, lights off most of the day. Someone rigged up a small TV. We huddled around it like it was a campfire.

The movie started. And within minutes, I understood why Dan had risked it.

Neo, trapped in a world that wasn't real. Morpheus offers the choice: red pill or blue pill. The truth or the illusion. Freedom or comfort.

"What if I told you," Morpheus said on-screen, "that everything you know is a lie?"

Someone in the back muttered, "Sounds about right."

We laughed—bitter, knowing laughter.

Because we got it.

We were living it.

The Matrix wasn't just a movie. It was a mirror. The halfway house, the ankle monitors, the supervision, the structure—all of it designed to keep us compliant, controlled, convinced that this was the only way forward.

But sitting there, slightly high, watching Neo choose the red pill and wake up to a reality he'd been blind to his entire life, I felt something crack open inside me.

What if this was the real prison?

Not the building. Not the rules. But the belief that I could only be one thing—either Mark, the manager who bagged fries and followed orders, or Ghost, the legend who burned too bright and crashed too hard.

What if there was a third option?

What if I could choose myself?

The credits rolled. The lights came back on. Dan grinned at me.

"Good shit, right?"

"Yeah," I said. But I wasn't talking about the movie.

* * *

Salary wage. Grease burns: early mornings and late nights.

Back where I grew up in Channelview, working at the same Burger King where I'd once performed birthday parties as Do Nut the clown—back when I was twelve, saving money for my first car, dreaming of freedom that looked nothing like what I'd eventually find.

The irony wasn't subtle.

At my return interview, the district manager leaned back in his chair and said, "You're the fastest rehire in company history." He said it like a compliment, but I heard what he didn't say: You fell so far you landed right back where you started.

And yet—I was good at this job.

Hell, I was great at it.

I treated my crew with respect. Kept things light but professional. Managed the madness of lunch rushes and late-night drunks with the same precision I'd once used to orchestrate nightclub lineups.

They trained me on the bell system—the one you'd ring to signal stock changes for the ready bin. Every time I rang it, muscle memory kicked in, and suddenly I'd hear it: that disco classic from my Village Station days echoing in my head. The beat. The joy. The freedom of a night when a bell meant celebration, not inventory.

Now it just meant we needed more Whoppers.

One afternoon at my original location—the store from my childhood, the one I knew by heart—I was managing the counter when I noticed one of my crew members getting harassed.

Erica.

We'd grown up together, played in the same neighborhood, and rode the same school bus. Seeing her behind that counter felt like looking at a mirror of who I might have been if the night had never found me.

Two customers were giving her hell—loud, aggressive, the entitled cruelty people reserve for service workers they've decided don't matter.

I stepped in.

"Ma'am," I said, voice calm but steel underneath, "you can take your business elsewhere. My staff and I expect to be spoken to with respect."

Another song bloomed in my mind—a different anthem, a different era, same message.

Something about respect.

They left.

Erica exhaled, her hands still shaking.

"Thank you," she said quietly.

"Always," I told her.

Because if the night had taught me anything, it was this: dignity isn't something you earn by being seen. It's something you claim by standing up for yourself, for your people, even when no one's watching.

Even when you're wearing a polyester uniform instead of platform shoes.

The customers saw a quiet guy behind the counter—older than the rest, maybe a little distant. They didn't know I'd once commanded rooms full of light and sound. They didn't know the same hands bagging fries had once painted spirals on my face, had once held the course of entire nights in their palms. And maybe that anonymity was what I needed.

To be no one.

To be still.

To learn that respect didn't require a spotlight.

Each paycheck felt like progress—small, quiet redemption. Each shift without drama was a brick in the foundation I was rebuilding. The work was honest in a way nothing else had been for years. No performance. No masks. Just showing up, doing the job, going home. There was something sacred in that monotony. Something I'd been running from my entire life. For the first time, I wasn't chasing anything.

I was just ... here.

Present.

Sober.

Alive.

* * *

House arrest taught me silence.

The first few weeks were the hardest. The walls seemed to breathe with memories—echoes of bass, laughter, and light that no longer belonged to me. Every reflection felt like a ghost of who I'd been.

143

I watched the world through glass, the streets and sky framed by window blinds. The nights were quiet, the kind of calm that presses down on you until you can hear your own thoughts arguing with themselves.

I've never been much for jewelry. To this day, I only wear a watch on occasion. Ornaments beyond sunglasses or the occasional neck chain were never my thing—no rings, no bracelets, no ankle beads.

So there was a certain irony—bitter and sharp—in the fact that the most significant piece of jewelry I'd ever worn was court-ordered.

The ankle monitor arrived the day I transitioned from the halfway house to house arrest. My probation officer came to my apartment with a black box and a clipboard, his expression somewhere between bored and apologetic.

"Don't get it wet," he said, kneeling to fit the device around my ankle. "Keep it charged. Report any outages immediately. Tampering will send you straight back to the county."

He snapped it into place.

Beep.

The sound was slight—innocuous, even—but it hit me like a gunshot.

That beep was my new reality.

Every hour, on the hour, the monitor would remind me: You are here. You are alive. You are not free.

After the probation officer left, I stood in front of the bathroom mirror, staring at my reflection. The person looking back was a stranger—no white face paint, no black spiral, no lightning bolt slashing across my cheek. Just Mark. Tired. Thin. Ordinary.

But as I stood there, something caught my eye.

Hanging on the back of the bathroom door was a yellow boa—forgotten, dusty, a relic from another life. And for just a second, I heard it: the opening notes of the Basement Jaxx remix of "Sesame Street," the crowd roaring, Paloma laughing, my voice shouting over the bass—

"Can you tell me how to get, how to get to Sesame Street?"

Big Bird Ghost. Paloma's birthday. Liquid. The night I knew I'd arrived.

The memory flickered like a candle in the wind. I looked back at the monitor clamped around my ankle, then back at the boa—two versions of myself, staring at each other across an impossible distance. I wasn't Ghost anymore. But I wasn't gone, either. Somewhere beneath the silence, beneath the fear and shame and exhaustion, there was still a glimmer. A spark. A stubborn, ridiculous refusal to believe this was the end.

I would find that light again.

I knew it.

I had to.

The first few weeks were the hardest. The apartment felt like a cage—not because it was small, but because I couldn't leave. Not for a walk. Not for air. Not even to drive aimlessly through the city at 2 a.m., the way I used to when my thoughts got too loud.

Every corner held a ghost: the couch where friends had crashed after all-night parties, the kitchen counter where I'd counted pills and planned DJ lineups, the window that once framed a city I owned.

Now the window framed a world I could only watch.

I'd stand there sometimes, blinds half-open, staring at the street below. Cars passed with bass thumping—muffled, distant, a rhythm I could no longer sync with. People walked by laughing, shouting, living. Friday nights, Saturday nights—they moved through the city like blood through veins while I stood still, a clot, a blockage, something the night had expelled.

The monitor beeped.

Every hour.

A mechanical heartbeat reminding me I was alive but not living.

Some nights I'd stare at it—this black plastic shackle—and think about all the other things that had held me captive over the years. Addiction. Attention. The desperate need to be seen. The night itself, with its promises and lies. The monitor was just more honest about it. At least now I could see my chains.

I learned to fill time differently. Reading. Writing. Thinking.

It was strange, having time that didn't revolve around nightfall.

* * *

When the monitor finally came off, the world didn't rush to greet me. It just ... waited.

Probation brought structure but also a kind of distance. I moved carefully, like someone relearning to walk. I had to check in, stay clean, stay quiet. The city looked familiar, but I no longer knew my place in it.

The old network was still out there—the DJs, promoters, party kids. I'd hear their names whispered sometimes, feel that familiar tug in my chest. But I stayed away.

For a while.

There was this emptiness, though—a hollow where the music used to live. I missed it: the lights, the noise—the belonging.

One night, I couldn't take it anymore.

The silence. The stillness. The hollow where the music used to live.

I drove downtown and found myself outside The Living Room—a new nightclub that had opened in the old Powertools space at 709 Franklin. I parked in the Commerce Street lot and stood there for a long moment, staring at the entrance.

Everything about downtown felt surreal that night.

The Franklin Road bridge loomed overhead. Chase Bank glowed across the street—closed, empty, corporate. A few blocks down, Kim Son restaurant's sign buzzed softly. Next door, the Magnolia Ballroom was hosting some kind of bridal event, tuxedos and white dresses visible through tall windows. On the corner, the brewery spilled golden light onto the sidewalk, laughter pouring out every time the door opened—cheers for a new generation.

And there, tucked beside it all, was the Spy Club—still standing, still glowing, a relic from the nights I used to rule.

But tonight, I wasn't going to Spy.

I was descending into something new.

The stairs down to The Living Room were the same stairs I'd walked a hundred times before—the stairs that had led down to Powertools, to those dark nights before Miami, before Ghost, before everything.

My feet knew every step by heart. But everything else had changed.

Inside, the industrial grit was gone. The Hernandez family—the same family I'd met years earlier in the Spy Club VIP lounge when they'd just signed the lease on this space—had transformed 709 Franklin into something sleek, warm, and inviting: couches instead of crates, curtains instead of exposed brick, soft golden lighting instead of harsh strobes. Pop house music pulsed through the space, melodic and clean—nothing like the dark, grinding bass Powertools used to shake through your chest.

They'd called it The Living Room.

And tonight, in my first week of sobriety, it felt like the only room in Houston where I could breathe.

It reminded me of Miami.

Not Salvation or Liquid—but the smaller lounges off Lincoln Road, the ones that felt expensive and exclusive without trying too hard. The vibe was sophisticated, curated, designed to make you feel like you'd stumbled into someone's impossibly cool private party.

At first, I blended in.

I moved to the music. Let the bass settle into my bones. Let the lights wash over me. For a few minutes, I almost felt like I belonged again—like I could slip back into this world without anyone noticing the gap, the absence, the year and a half I'd spent locked away.

And then I saw her.

At the bar, golden under the low lighting, eyeliner sharp enough to cut, face painted for the gods.

Alecia.

She sat on a stool nursing a martini, one leg crossed over the other, exuding the same effortless glamour she'd had back at the Regency Hotel in South Beach—the night we'd met, the night Ted introduced me to the velvet machine, the night I first stepped into a world I thought would never let me go.

My heart kicked.

I shouldn't have approached. But that is not who I am.

I should have turned around, walked back up those stairs, driven home, and accepted that some doors close permanently.

But I didn't.

I walked to the bar.

She didn't turn at first. Didn't acknowledge me. Just took a slow sip of her drink, her reflection shimmering in the mirror behind the bottles.

"Alecia," I said quietly.

She turned then—slowly, deliberately—and looked me up and down. Not the way you look at an old friend. The way you look at a ghost you'd rather not see.

Her expression didn't shift. No smile. No surprise. No warmth. Just cold recognition.

"I know who you are," she said flatly.

Five words.

That was it.

No "How have you been?"

No, "I heard what happened."

No acknowledgment of the years we'd spent orbiting the same world, the same parties, the same impossible dream.

"I know who you are."

As if my presence had ruined her anonymous placement, precluding her involvement and any connection to the South Beach scene at all. Ended her night and reminded her of a version of Miami—of herself—that she'd worked hard to forget.

I was the Ghost at the feast. The reminder that everything golden eventually tarnishes.

"Good to see you," I managed, my voice thin.

She turned back to her drink without another word.

I stood there for a beat longer than I should have—waiting for something, anything, some small thread of connection to prove that the past had mattered.

But there was nothing.

Just the music. The lights. The crowd was moving around us like we didn't exist.

I walked away.

Found a corner. Finished my drink. Watched the room pulse and breathe without me.

No one else recognized me either.

Not one person.

I had spent years building a name, a presence, a legend—and now I was invisible.

The Living Room wouldn't stay that way for long. Within months, it would be rebranded and opened under the name Rehab, and I'd find my way back into the machinery. But that night, standing in the shadows of a space I used to know, I understood something I hadn't before:

Ghost wasn't just a costume I could put back on.

He was a currency. And I was bankrupt.

But as I stood there under the strobes, something stirred—faint, stubborn, refusing to die. That old rhythm. That hum in my bones.

I wasn't ready to step back in. Not yet.

But I would be.

Because once you've been Ghost, the night never really lets you go.

14

Ghost Town

By the time I finished probation, I'd rebuilt something inside myself.

The ankle monitor came off on a Tuesday afternoon. The technician who'd strapped it on months earlier returned to remove it, flipping the clasp open with the same mechanical efficiency he'd used to lock it in place.

No ceremony. No congratulations. Just a nod and a reminder to keep my nose clean.

I walked him to the door, closed it behind him, and stood in the silence of my apartment. For the first time in eighteen months, I was free. Sort of.

Ghost was still there, buried beneath the uniform and the schedules and the daily grind. Quieter now. Deeper. Patient. Waiting.

But for the first time in years, Mark was breathing again.

I told myself the past was behind me.

That the silence was safety.

That I could build a life in daylight and leave the night where it belonged, behind glass, behind memory, behind the version of myself I'd barely survived.

* * *

Back on the east side in my self-regulated exile.

The phone started ringing. Not often at first--whispers from old friends, tentative invitations, questions about whether I was back or just visiting.

And the whispers began to sound like destiny.

I wasn't sure if it was fate or temptation calling me home. But I knew what was coming. One night, I answered.

It was NutZ calling me, a DJ I'd known from the old days.

"Are you ready to come back?" he asked over the phone. "Because we've got something new, something big."

After we hung up, I stood in my apartment, staring at the closet where I'd shoved everything months ago, back when I thought Ghost was dead, back when I thought Mark could survive on his own.

I pulled out the cardboard box.

Dust had settled on the lid like snow. I brushed it off and opened it slowly, the cardboard creaking like a door I'd nailed shut.

Inside: the costumes from South Beach.

Leopard-print platform shoes. Maroon ones. The black-and-white pair that had carried me through a hundred nights. Six-inch Demonia platforms with buckles that still gleamed. Non-distributed "Romper Room" fliers from the disaster at Salvation--evidence of failure I'd never thrown away.

Bart Simpson's molded hair.

Yellow and red boas shedding feathers like memories.

A Caboodles kit, complete with clown makeup, now cracked and dried.

A dozen backpacks: the one-of-a-kind Kabuki, the stoplight, several '80s-style lunchboxes I'd carried like armor.

The box smelled like dust, old glitter and something else I couldn't name.

Possibility, maybe.

Or ghosts.

I reached in and pulled out one platform shoe—the leopard-print one, my favorite. I slipped it on.

It still fit.

I stood, wobbling slightly, and caught my reflection in the mirror. One platform shoe. Sweatpants. A T-shirt from a life I was supposed to be living.

I looked ridiculous.

But I also looked ... right.

NutZ's words echoed: "The venue's called Nsomnia."

I'd laughed when he said it. Nsomnia. The universe's cruel little joke—a club named after sleeplessness, after nights that refuse to end, after the thing I'd been running from and toward my entire life.

But deep down, I knew it wasn't a coincidence. The world was calling me back, daring me to rebuild from the ashes.

Part of me wanted to throw it all away. Burn the box. Bury Ghost for good. But another part—the part that still heard bass in my bones—knew the truth:

Ghost wasn't gone.

He was waiting.

I wasn't the same Ghost anymore. I couldn't be. The boy who'd walked into Heaven at sixteen, the wannabe legend who'd worked South Beach, the fool who'd crashed and burned—those versions were gone.

But maybe that was okay.

Maybe Ghost could evolve.

Maybe he had to.

The scene that had destroyed me was the only place I'd ever truly belonged.

I took a breath.

Pulled out my phone.

Called NutZ back.

"I'm in," I said.

And just like that, the haunting began again.

* * *

Throughout my time on probation, I built a life.

Boring, maybe. But stable.

Weekdays at Burger King, then later Wendy's after a better offer came through. I managed lunch rushes and inventory counts, hired teenagers who showed up late and called in sick on Saturdays, and dealt with angry customers who thought a wrong order was the end of the world.

I was good at it. The same skills that had once helped me read a nightclub crowd—anticipating needs, managing chaos, keeping things moving—translated perfectly to fast-food management. District managers praised my numbers. Crew members respected me. I had health insurance, a pension, and a name tag that said "Mark" in block letters.

I rented a small house down the street from my parents. They were protective—understandably so, given everything I--and they--had been through. Sunday dinners became routine. My mother would make pot roast. My stepdad would ask about work. Neither of them mentioned platforms or face paint or the fact that I'd once been somebody people whispered about in rooms I no longer entered.

On the surface, I was Mark Stevens: assistant manager, good son, reformed.

But underneath, something else was stirring.

Friday nights were the hardest.

I'd be home by seven, showered and changed, standing in my small living room, wondering what to do with the hours stretching ahead. The city outside my windows would start to come alive. And I'd feel it. That old ache. That hunger.

I'd catch myself staring at the closet where I'd shoved the cardboard box months ago--the one I'd sealed shut the day the ankle monitor came off, promising myself I was done.

Done with Ghost. Done with the chaos. Done chasing light that always burned out.

But my fingers would itch for white face paint. My feet would remember the weight of six-inch platforms--the way they made me taller, bolder, untouchable. My body would crave the bass--not just hearing it, but feeling it move through my chest like a second heartbeat.

Some nights I'd drive. Just drive. Windows down, radio off, cruising past the old spots. Heaven was closed now, the building dark, windows boarded up like a tomb. Rich's still stood on Brazos, but the energy was different. The faces outside were younger, hungrier, chasing something they didn't have names for yet.

I'd park down the street and watch. Just watch. Telling myself I was only curious, only checking in, only seeing what had changed.

But deep down, I knew the truth.

The night was calling.

And I was running out of reasons to say no.

Saturday mornings, I'd wake up feeling hollow, like I'd spent the whole night holding my breath. I'd go to work, flip burgers, count registers, smile at customers, and pretend that this was enough.

That Mark was enough.

That Ghost could stay buried forever.

But the box in the closet kept whispering.

And eventually, the phone rang.

I began going out to Montrose again sporadically. It was during one of these trips to the Guava Lamp that I met Magick——a club promoter working with Madam Pussycat and promoting parties with a club-kid flair!

Excited to be back in the flow of things, I remember suggesting to Magick that we look for a place to rent.

To my parents' strict objection, I moved back inside the loop.

It wasn't long before I was partying and missing work, and I decided to quit to go back to promoting full-time, no funny business this time, only promoting, and some partying.

I abandoned the east side for a downstairs apartment off of Cullen Avenue, not far from the University of Houston main campus, and just around the corner from Mrs. Baird's bakery.

As you can imagine, the aroma from the bakery was heavenly.

* * *

In my early days as a raver, club-hopping from Heaven to the after-hours at Club Some, there were specific landmarks we'd pass along the way, places that glowed in the periphery, mysterious and inviting but never quite the destination. One of them sat at 202 Tuam Avenue. Back then, it was called The Magic Bus.

I'd driven past it a hundred times, windows down, my head turned just enough to catch the neon sign and wonder what went on inside. It always seemed alive—lights flickering, shadows moving behind frosted glass, but I'd never stopped.

Until now.

Years later, after everything had burned down and rebuilt itself, I found myself standing in front of that same building. The sign was different. The name had changed. But the energy was the same.

This time, I wasn't passing by.

This time, I was walking in.

I met the manager on a humid afternoon, the kind where Houston's air feels thick enough to chew. He was older, soft-spoken, with a type of weariness that comes from fighting battles most people don't see.

He told me the story:

The venue had been launched by a nonprofit dedicated to HIV and AIDS research. In a city—a community—still reeling from the losses of the 1980s and '90s, this club was a sanctuary in more ways than one. A bring-your-own-alcohol experience where you purchased soda or orange juice and made your own cocktails.

"We're looking for someone to bring in a crowd," he said, studying me carefully. "Someone who understands what this means."

I understood.

I'd watched an entire generation disappear. I'd danced in rooms full of men who wouldn't live to see thirty. I'd stood beside Kitty and Paloma as they fought—through performance, through visibility, through sheer refusal to be erased—for a community under siege.

This wasn't just another party.

This was a cause I could stand behind.

"I'll take the door," I said. "Cover charge, DJ, entertainment—I'll handle it."

He extended his hand.

"Saturdays are yours."

A few weeks later, I was back in my apartment, sitting cross-legged on the floor with my roommate, Magick, and his best friend, Lexi Peppermint.

We were planning.

"We need a name," Magick said, flipping through a notebook covered in doodles and half-formed ideas.

"Something that feels safe," Lexi added. "But also ... alive."

I thought about Heaven. About Club Some. About all the places that had saved me before I knew I needed saving.

"Sanctuary," I said.

They both looked up.

"Sanctuary Saturdays."

Lexi grinned. "Perfect."

But before I could step back into that world—before I could stand at a door and invite people into something I'd built—I needed one thing:

The shoes.

Ghost didn't exist without platforms.

I took a pair of black tennis shoes to the boot-repair shop on Uvalde in Northshore—the same neighborhood where I'd most recently been a general manager for Wendy's, flipping between daylight and the dream of something more.

The cobbler was a Hispanic transplant from Mexico——stoic, unimpressed by my request.

"Six inches," I said. "Foam layers. Slanted grade for balance."

He raised an eyebrow.

"You gonna be able to walk in these?"

"I've done it before," I said.

He shrugged and got to work.

A week later, I picked them up. They were perfect—monstrous, ridiculous, precisely what I needed. I slipped them on in the parking lot and stood, wobbling slightly.

I looked down at my feet—elevated, transformed, powerful.

Ghost was back.

The first night of Sanctuary, I arrived early. The Magic Bus—now repurposed, reborn—glowed softly under the streetlights. Inside, the space was raw but welcoming: exposed brick, string lights, a small bar, a dance floor just big enough to hold a crowd without crushing it.

DJ NutZ was already setting up, headphones around his neck and a crate of records at his feet.

"You ready?" he asked.

I adjusted my platform and checked my reflection in a window.

White face paint. Black spiral on my right cheek. Lightning bolt across my left.

The uniform hadn't changed.

But the man wearing it had.

"Yeah," I said. "I'm ready."

By midnight, the room was alive.

Bodies pressed against each other, sweat and laughter, and the kind of joy that only happens when people feel safe enough to let go. The bass rolled through the floor. The lights flickered in time with the beat. Strangers became friends. Friends became family.

My evil twin, you might say, Lexi was often my muse during the performance-art parts of my weekly parties. I once dropped a cardboard chimney on her head to the song "Feel It."

And I stood at the door, collecting covers, greeting faces.

This was different from before.

I wasn't performing for the crowd.

I was creating space for them.

At some point in the night, Magick found me by the door, grinning. "We are at capacity! Don't let anyone else in!"

By the time the night ended, the sun was threatening the horizon.

I stood in the empty club, platforms kicked off, face paint smeared, exhausted in the best way.

DJ NutZ was packing up his crates.

"That was good," he said. "Real good."

I nodded.

It had been.

Not because it was wild, dangerous, or legendary.

But because it was honest.

Because it mattered.

Ghost had returned.

But this time, he wasn't chasing the spotlight.

He was building something worth remembering.

Everything was set.

* * *

The first night I started promoting again, I realized how different things had become, as many of the past venues were now closed.

I was no longer the spectacle—I was the conductor.

Negotiating with club owners. Planning lineups. Booking a DJ and designing fliers. Every detail mattered. Every word on the phone, every text, every promise could make or break a night. The crowd's energy wasn't an accident anymore—it was a reflection of the work done behind the scenes.

Some nights were pure magic.

I remember one Thursday at a midtown lounge—the bass hit so hard the glasses trembled, and lights sliced through fog like slow lightning. I stood by the bar, watching it unfold, knowing I had built this moment—curated every sound, every flicker of light. That pride was not just from being seen, but from creating something worth seeing.

Other nights were harder—lessons in humility and control.

One Saturday, the DJ I'd booked called an hour before doors—his equipment had been stolen from his car. I stood in my apartment, platforms already on, face paint half-done, trying not to panic. I called every DJ I knew, begging for favors.

DJ NutZ saved me that night, showing up thirty minutes before midnight with his crates and a grin.

"You owe me," he said.

"Forever," I promised.

The crowd never knew how close we'd come to disaster. They danced until dawn while I stood by the door with my heart still racing. That's when I learned: the magic the crowd sees isn't what happens on the floor—it's what you prevent from happening in the first place.

Promoters fought over tables, DJs had egos bigger than the room, and owners demanded miracles on budgets that barely covered barbacks. But I learned the rhythm of business, how to read people before they spoke, how to sense the shift in energy before the night turned.

The faces of the past—Munday, Star, Boy Wonder, and Daydream—had long faded into memory, replaced by new collaborators and dreamers like Magick and Lexi Peppermint. Together, we built nights that had their own language, their own wild light.

* * *

Through Magick and Lexi, I met Jason, my boyfriend at the time, and one of the most important people in my life.

But that meeting didn't happen the way most love stories do. Jason was from the east side, like me. He'd been hanging out with a girl named Sunny, who was obsessed with Magick.

The details are fuzzy.

At one after-hours party at my house, a guy named Wilson showed up—a random Cling-On nobody really knew. NutZ was there too. Somehow, Wilson and Jason started dating. I was furious—I'd had my eye on Jason since the moment Magick introduced us. But it was short-lived. A few weeks later, Jason and Wilson broke up.

A few weeks later, while we were setting up for Sanctuary, Magick called me over.

"There's someone you need to meet," he said.

He led me through the empty club to where Lexi was holding court near the bar. And there, leaning against the wall with a shy smile and curious eyes, was Jason.

He was slim, attractive in a way that didn't demand attention but quietly earned it. Dark hair, artistic hands, wearing a vintage Go-Go's T-shirt and jeans that looked like they'd been painted on. But it was his eyes that caught me—kind, curious, searching for something real in a world full of performance.

"This is my friend," Magick said with a knowing grin. "He wanted to check out what you're building."

Jason extended his hand. "I've heard a lot about you," he said.

I shook his hand, felt the spark. "Good things, I hope."

He smiled. "We'll see."

Magick and Lexi drifted away—suspiciously convenient—leaving us alone in the empty club. The silence stretched, but it wasn't awkward. It was curious. Waiting.

"So," Jason said, looking around the space. "You're throwing some unique parties here?"

"Trying," I said. "Not sure if I'm succeeding."

"Why here?" he asked. "Why this place?"

I told him about the nonprofit. "This isn't just a party," I said. "It's a sanctuary. Literally. The money goes to keeping people alive."

Jason nodded slowly, taking that in. "That's why you came back," he said. "Not for the spotlight. For the cause."

I blinked. Most people assumed I came back because I was an addict—addicted to attention, to chaos, to the night itself. But Jason had seen past that in five minutes.

"Yeah," I said quietly. "For the cause."

He smiled—not the performative smile I was used to seeing in clubs, but something genuine. Warm.

"I'm from the east side," he said. "Crosby area. Worked at a grocery store for three years, saving money to move into the city. My family didn't understand why I had to leave. Why I couldn't just ... be normal."

"I know that feeling," I said.

"I know you do," he said. "That's why Magick thought we should meet."

We talked for an hour—about the east side neighborhoods we both grew up in, about what it meant to escape and what it cost to come back. About art and music and the difference between performing for others and creating for yourself.

He didn't ask about Ghost, the legend. He didn't care about platform shoes or face paint or the nights I'd spent ruling South Beach.

He was interested in Mark—the person underneath, the one who still wasn't sure if he was allowed to exist.

That was new.

That was terrifying.

That was precisely what I needed.

"You should come back next week," I said as we were leaving.

"I'd like that," he said.

* * *

The following Saturday, he stayed over.

There was tension, the wanting, the unspoken question of what we were and where this was going.

But that night, something shifted. We were in my tiny kitchen, cleaning up after dinner. I was at the sink, washing dishes, and he came up behind me, hands on my waist, lips on my neck. "Hey," he whispered. I turned, soap still on my hands, and kissed him. It wasn't like the frantic, desperate encounters I'd had before—quick, fueled by drugs and adrenaline.

This was slow. Deliberate. Real. He lifted me onto the counter, and I wrapped my legs around him. Amber's "Sexual" was playing from someone's open window down the street, the bass drifting through the summer air, and it felt like the universe was scoring this moment specifically for us.

"Is this okay?" he asked.

"Yeah," I said. "It's okay."

We moved to the bedroom, and for once, I wasn't performing. I wasn't Ghost. I wasn't trying to be anything other than exactly who I was—scars, mistakes, and all.

Afterward, we lay tangled in sheets, the fan overhead doing its best to fight the Houston heat. He traced circles on my chest, silent, thoughtful.

"What are you thinking?" I asked.

"That I don't want this to end."

"It doesn't have to."

He looked at me, and there was something in his eyes—hope, maybe, or fear. "You say that now. But I know what the night means to you."

"The night doesn't mean anything if I lose this," I said. And I meant it. In that moment, I meant it. But somewhere deep down, I knew the truth: the night wasn't done with me yet. And when it called again—and it would—I'd have to choose.

I didn't know yet that I'd make the wrong choice.

* * *

He showed up the following Saturday. And the Saturday after that. And the one after that.

Within a week, we were having breakfast together after the club closed—sitting in a 24-hour diner on Westheimer, still buzzing from the night, watching the sun come up over a city that felt newly possible.

Within two weeks, he'd left a toothbrush at my apartment.

Within a month, he'd moved in.

Not because of attraction—though that was there too, electric and undeniable—but because we understood each other in a way I'd never experienced before.

Jason didn't want to fix me. He didn't want to save me. He didn't want to turn me into a different version of Mark or turn me back into Ghost.

He just wanted to be with me. Whoever I was. Whoever I was becoming.

For the first time in my life, that felt like enough.

Jason was one of the kindest and most caring people I have ever met.

I drove to bring him to club nights a few times, and he would stay the night each time. He was there helping me plan the opening of Nsomnia and had moved in with me.

We were inseparable.

On Mondays and Tuesdays—the only nights Sanctuary was dark—we'd collapse into bed and stay there for hours. Not just sleeping. Just ... being. Talking. Laughing. Tracing patterns on each other's skin while the city happened outside the windows.

I can remember one particular Tuesday afternoon, early spring, when neither of us had anywhere to be. We'd been together about two months by then—he'd been living with me for one. Jason was sketching at the kitchen table. I was working on fliers for the upcoming nights—trying to design something eye-catching on a budget that barely covered paper and ink.

I'd been stressed all week. Numbers were down. The nonprofit manager had called, asking why cover charges were dropping.

A rival promoter had started a competing night at a bigger venue. I was worried the magic wouldn't work this time. Worried I'd fail again, the way I'd failed at Romper Room in Miami, the way I'd failed at everything that mattered.

Jason looked up from his drawing. "You know it's going to be okay, right?"

"How do you know?" I asked, not looking up from the computer.

He put down his pencil. Walked over. Turned my chair around so I had to face him.

"Because you care," he said. "That's the difference between you and everyone else out there. You actually give a shit. You're not doing this for fame or money or attention. You're doing it because it matters."

I felt something crack open in my chest—not the rush of the night, but something quieter. Deeper. Scarier.

"What if caring isn't enough?" I asked.

"It's always enough," he said.

He reached down, took my hands, and pulled me up from the chair. Led me to the couch. We lay there for hours—him sketching, me planning, Amber's "Sexual" playing on repeat from the CD player because I was too lazy to get up and change it.

"De de da de, da da de …"

The song became our soundtrack. Our rhythm. The sound of safety.

"This is the only time in my life I've felt this," I said at some point, half-asleep against his chest.

"Felt what?" he asked.

"Like I don't have to be anyone. Like Mark is enough. Like I don't need Ghost to matter."

He kissed the top of my head. "You've always mattered," he said. "You just didn't know it yet."

I wanted to freeze that moment. Bottle it. Keep it forever.

But even then, I could feel the night pulling at the edges—whispering that this peace was temporary, that Ghost was waiting, that the silence would eventually become unbearable.

I didn't realize just how soon.

While collecting actual, legitimate party supplies at the local store off of Studemont, Jason and I met Faye. She was the director of the event center behind the store. Faye was a champion of what we were doing and often helped me find good deals on piñatas, cotton-candy machines, and other props for the weekly parties at Sanctuary, then Rehab and beyond.

When it was time for us to move out of the Cullen apartment, Faye suggested we move in next to him, since the complex was only five minutes from the club. We did, and things were smooth for a period.

Faye even bought me a Star Trek cutout of Captain Janeway for Christmas that year. She holds a special place in my heart for always looking after Jason and me during this time.

On mornings when I'd come home from the club exhausted, makeup smeared, still wearing platforms, Faye would be on her porch with coffee and a smile—never judging, constantly checking that we were okay.

V

Phoenix

Houston, 2000–1. Ghost returned home not as a legend, but as a survivor trying to rebuild. Through Sanctuary, through Rehab, through one last attempt at glory, he learned that resurrection doesn't mean returning to who you were—it means becoming someone new. This is the story of second chances and final falls, of discovering that the night can't save you forever, and that sometimes the bravest thing you can do is stop running. Twenty-five years later, Ghost finally rests.

15

Rehab

By the start of the New Year in 2000, Houston's nightlife had changed—and so had I.

The wild, chaotic nights of my club kid youth weren't entirely behind me, but I was stepping into a new role: one that demanded vision, strategy, and nerves of steel.

This chapter of my life is named "Rehab," though it wasn't a detox from drugs or alcohol. It was a detox from aimlessness—from being swept along by the scene instead of steering it. I was learning to channel the chaos I once embodied into something lasting. I wasn't just living for the night anymore; I was building it.

However, by the end of 2000, the city was undergoing another transformation.

The parties were starting to return.

New venues.

New names.

New DJs spinning the same old hunger into fresh beats. Not long after Sanctuary launched, I got a call that would change everything.

Word had spread that the old Powertools space, later The Living Room, the same address, that had tested me as a teenager, the same concrete walls that had once dripped with sweat and rebellion.

The club was called Rehab.

I called the info line out of curiosity.

A voice answered—smooth, professional, radio-perfect:

"This weekend at Club Rehab: drink specials and no cover before midnight."

Something about that voice snagged in my memory. I'd heard it before—years ago, on the radio, back when I was sneaking into clubs with a fake ID, back when disco nights at the Tower Theater – a relic of 1950s Art Deco, similar to what I had been surrounded by in Miami, and central to the Montrose and Westheimer neighborhoods for decades – felt like the most sophisticated thing Houston had to offer.

Chris Alan. The DJ. He was a Houston legend. And now he was opening a club.

I left a message.

Then another.

Finally, he called back.

"I've heard about you," he said, his voice carrying that same FM smoothness in person. "Let's meet. I'm doing liquor delivery tomorrow afternoon. Come by around 3:00."

I showed up at 2:45, too nervous to be late, too excited to wait in the car.

The staff entrance was round back—an unmarked door next to a loading dock, the kind reserved for employees and people who belonged. I'd never walked through this door before. At Powertools, I'd always come in through the front, just another body in the crowd.

But now?

Now I was walking in during daylight hours, invited, expected.

I felt powerful.

I wore my black platform-heel shoes――not the towering six-inch monsters I'd had custom-made. These were different, not the towering six-inch monsters of my wildest nights. These were different. Refined. Elevated but controlled.

Classy Ghost, if there ever was one.

I'd dressed carefully: black pants, a fitted shirt, minimal makeup. I wanted to look like someone who could build a brand, not just someone who embodied chaos. I brought a folder of fliers from Miami—my Romper Room disaster, a few Liquid nights, proof that I'd been part of something bigger than Houston.

Proof that I knew how to dream.

Inside, the transformation was stunning.

Powertools had been stripped down to its bones and rebuilt into something sleek, surreal, almost otherworldly. The concrete walls were painted in deep purples and blacks. Hundreds of black lights lined the ceiling. Mushrooms and spirals covered the walls—psychedelic, hypnotic, alive.

The DJ booth sat elevated in the center of the main room, encased in glass. It looked like a rave had been injected into a nightclub and left to mutate into something beautiful.

Chris Alan stood near the bar, clipboard in hand, checking off bottles as they were unloaded. He looked up when I walked in.

"You must be Ghost," he said, extending a hand.

I shook it. "And you're the voice from the radio," I said.

He smiled—not surprised, just pleased I'd noticed.

"Guilty."

We sat at the bar while the delivery crew worked around us. I spread my fliers across the counter like tarot cards, each one a piece of the story I was trying to tell.

He barely glanced at them. Instead, he looked at me.

"You know," he said, leaning back, "you could be the Michael Alig of Houston."

The words hit me like a spotlight.

I laughed—half-flattered, half-wary.

"Let's hope without the manslaughter," I said.

He grinned. "Fair."

But I knew what he meant.

By then, *Disco Bloodbath*—the book about Michael Alig and the original club kids—had been released. The movie *Party Monster* was in development. The scene that had once been underground, exclusive, and magical was now infamous. The world knew the names: Michael, James St. James, Amanda Lepore. They knew the glamour. They knew the tragedy.

And Chris saw that same energy in me—the ability to turn nightlife into theatre, to make a room feel like an event just by being there.

It was thrilling.

It was also terrifying.

Because I knew how that story ended.

"Look," Chris said, pulling my attention back. "I'm not asking you to be him. I'm asking you to be you. But bigger. Focused. Houston needs this energy again."

He gestured to the space around us

"We're building something here. Something that matters. And I think you could be part of it."

I nodded, my eyes drifting across the walls.

That's when I saw it.

The logo.

Behind the bar, painted in bold letters across the brick: REHAB.

And rippling through the word, woven into the design like DNA, was a spiral—the same spiral I'd been painting on my face for years.

My signature.

My symbol.

The universal sign for life, movement, galaxies, hurricanes—everything I'd ever tried to embody.

It was already here.

Waiting for me.

I pointed at it.

"That spiral," I said quietly. "I've been wearing that on my face since I became Ghost."

Chris followed my gaze and smiled.

We spent the next hour laying out a plan.

"I want you on the team," Chris said. "Promoter. Host. Whatever you want to call it. Bring your people. Build your nights."

I thought about Sanctuary. About the nonprofit. About the slower, steadier work I'd been doing.

This was different.

This was bigger.

This was Rehab.

"I'm in," I said.

We shook hands.

As I stood to leave, an idea sparked.

"I want to do themed nights," I said. "Rehab-themed. Medical. Performance art."

Chris raised an eyebrow.

"Like what?"

"E=mergency," I said. "Visiting Hours. Promotions dressed as doctors and nurses. Prescriptions for the party. Make it immersive."

He grinned.

"I love it. Do it."

I walked out through that same staff entrance, the afternoon sun blinding after the darkness inside.

My platforms clicked against the pavement. In my hand, I carried the folder of old fliers—evidence of who I'd been. But in my chest, something new was building. Not just a comeback. A resurrection.

Ghost wasn't returning to the scene he'd left.

He was building a new one.

And this time, the spiral wasn't just painted on my face.

It was carved into the walls.

That day, I joined Club Rehab as part of the team. But more than that, I found purpose again.

* * *

The grand opening fell on Halloween weekend—perfect timing for Ghost's return. As part of my first official duties as a club promoter, I hosted my first-ever costume contest.

Rehab occupied the space that had once held Powertools at 709 Franklin

Avenue, just off Main Street and around the corner from the Spy Club—the same club I had visited a few years earlier, the one often credited with bringing nightlife back downtown from the Richmond Strip and southwest Houston.

Rehab had been transformed with hundreds of black lights. The club's logo fit perfectly with the spiral I wore as part of my iconic Ghost makeup. First prize for the costume contest was a car painted to match the club's neon aesthetic.

We held the contest, and the winner showed up dressed as Paul McCartney from The Beatles. Ironically, they were actually from England, accent and all—meaning they had no way to take the 1989 Ford Contour home, especially not one covered in a neon spiral Rehab logo across the back window and hood.

Since the car matched the club perfectly, I offered them $300 cash and bought it on the spot.

I immediately put it to work, driving around town, passing out fliers, and building hype for the club. Everywhere we went, people stopped us to ask, "What's Rehab?" (Later, I even used the car to visit Kitty when she came to town for the Combustion circuit party.)

*　*　*

After the Halloween weekend, I began getting the word out, handing out fliers, and primarily promoting Club Rehab.

On Friday and Saturday nights, I dressed in full club kid regalia—platform tennis shoes, wild makeup, and a doctor's lab coat—and pranced down Main Street flanked by two blonde bombshells with perfect figures, both wearing nurse's hats and skimpy nurse outfits. I handed out "prescriptions" to people I met.

Much like the label printer I used years earlier on South Beach, these prescriptions were little slips that assigned each person their cure: *No Line, No Cover, One Free Shot at the Bar*, or, for a select few, *Please Don't Ever Come to Our Club.*

Chris used to say I was "Pied Piper Ghost" during this time, because I'd leave to promote and come back to Rehab with a trail of partygoers following behind me, ready for a taste of the underground magic.

One Thursday night stands out. Sebastian (Paris, London), Mikie Pratt—the same DJ from STEAM who'd warned me about chaos years ago—and I had marched up and down San Jacinto, drifting through other clubs and luring their patrons back to Rehab. By closing time, we had emptied several venues.

When the lights came up, Chris Alan pointed to the floor, laughing—layers of orange, pink, and red wristbands from rival clubs were scattered everywhere, shed by people the moment they walked into ours.

* * *

Being located at 709 Franklin, Rehab was still somewhat remote in the early 2000s. There were no nearby shops or convenience stores, and I began to notice a pattern: people looked like they were starving, desperate for snacks, or in dire need of cigarettes. The bartenders kept one carton behind the bar, but it often ran out, leaving patrons to drive nearly five miles to the closest mini-mart off I-10 and Studemont. That 24-hour Chevron always had a line stretching out the door, and it was the only place close enough that someone could make the trip and still get back to the club within an hour.

So I hatched a plan. I approached Chris Alan and said, "Hey, can we use that old bar space near the entrance to open a small shop and coat check?" He was thrilled by the idea and immediately agreed.

We opened the window and cleaned out the dusty space, setting up a small display of candy, cigarettes, and snacks. The only hassle was a leaking pipe in the back—one I prayed was coming from the bar upstairs, not the restrooms.

Club management gave me $500, and I headed to Sam's Club to stock up, stopping first at Flux Graphics in Montrose to pick up the "Visiting Hours" fliers. It was during coat-check days that Lexi brought in one of their friends, Steven Lawrence. He was dating a young blond bombshell named Kay Kay, who was sweet and full of life, a raver girl to the core at the time, and they became good friends of Jason and mine. We would eventually collaborate on a few events and move into the apartment complex above them on the southwest side of Houston, off of Westheimer Street. Steven would go on to become a very successful DJ, first as part of the duo Lawrence & Celauro and then as part of the group Tr3n.

* * *

Chris Alan had given me $500 to stock the Rehab shop, so the plan was simple: grab the fliers, then head to Sam's Club for snacks and cigarettes. First, Jason and I stopped at Flux, which was located above the vintage-clothing store Wear It Again Sam—the same place where I'd bought my first pair of platform shoes.

When we walked into the space, one of my old-school promoter friends was already there—one of the promoters I had known from my prior days in Houston, Nathan, from a promotional crew I was friendly with and cross-promoted with. This crew was primarily known for parties for Mitch Burman: rock-star club owner of the downtown venue named the Engine Room. A few other promoters were hanging around as well.

About five minutes after we arrived, someone burst into the office with a Glock 9 and demanded all our valuables. They didn't hesitate—they left with watches, cigarettes, credit cards, and the $500 I had been given to shop for the club.

Later that evening, back at Faye's apartment, I was distraught. I had no idea what to do, especially because the perpetrator was known to the owners of Flux. I was told they would "deal with it," but that brought me no comfort. Faye was right when she insisted that I at least file a police report, if only to preserve my credibility with the owners of Rehab.

So I followed her advice. We met with the Houston Police Department outside the Flux offices, and Faye came along for support. While we were giving the report, one of the owners arrived and confirmed everything, apologizing for not acting sooner.

I informed the owners of Rehab about the robbery, but the damage had been done. From that point forward, I was never trusted with club money again. As expected, they were disappointed—but to their credit, they still helped me get everything we needed to launch the Shop & Coat Check at Club Rehab.

Despite the rocky beginning, the shop turned out to be a resounding success.

* * *

Once Rehab heated up and became the go-to after-hours spot, it wasn't uncommon to see celebrities in the club. Honestly, Chris Alan and Zack Truesdell were celebrities in their own right—both coming from the music and radio industries. Zack was one-third of the hip-hop group Knight & Dae and a successful entrepreneur, and Chris had photos with Snoop Dogg, Sting, and countless others. Rehab was Houston's first official hip-hop club, and that alone—combined with the owners' reputations—gave performers and DJs even more reason to show up and show out.

This became the norm: DJ FLEX spinning in the main room, me hosting, and house or techno DJs filling the entrance room. Because my background and preference were always house and techno, I was often unaware when famous rappers came through. I only perked up when an R&B diva who'd lent her voice to a house track appeared—artists like Ultra Naté, Mary J. Blige, or Deborah Cox. Those were the moments I lived for.

So you can imagine my confusion on an especially packed Saturday night when several "up-and-coming artists" arrived at the club. Saturdays at Rehab were different from any other night—we doubled security, and the owners' moms and dads worked the cover window. That night, Ricky Ross, one of our main bouncers, called me urgently to the front door and asked me to escort a group to the VIP area in the main room.

As I approached the entrance, Mrs. Hernandez caught my eye and mouthed,

"Don't fuck this up," then pointed toward a small entourage waiting off to the side.

Ricky leaned in and whispered, "Get these girls to the DJ booth—they're about to play one of their new releases."

I was wearing my four-inch platforms that night, so the girls seemed unusually short to me. The upside was that the shoes let me see above the sea of bodies as I mapped out the fastest route through the crowd. DJ FLEX was waving frantically for me to hurry, pointing toward the VIP lounge beside his turntables.

It wasn't until we were halfway through the crowd that it hit me: I was escorting Beyoncé and Kelly Rowland of Destiny's Child to the DJ booth so they could premiere "Bills, Bills, Bills" before the single officially dropped.

Both of them were kind, gracious, and grounded. Beyoncé smiled and thanked me, and Kelly even told me I embodied the New York club kid aesthetic. She laughed and added, "I thought for sure you were the queen of this club."

She wasn't wrong.

* * *

Rehab was more than a club; it was a machine—a living ecosystem of lights, sound, and emotion. We built nights that thrummed with intention. From DJ lineups to lighting cues, from guest lists to after-parties, nothing happened by accident. Everything was engineered to feel effortless.

The name might have suggested recovery, but inside, it was pure release—a place where people came to lose themselves, find themselves, and become someone new before sunrise. In the middle of that controlled chaos, I found my own balance.

We lived for the spectacle. By Friday night, the entrance set the tone: an illuminated archway wrapped in the Rehab logo's neon spiral. You descended the stairs to the ticket booth, and directly ahead sat the coat check—my little kingdom of candy, cigarettes, and late-night confessions.

To the right was the front-room DJ booth, then another arch leading into the smaller main room, with its lowered dance floor and metal railings. In those early days, a bar sat in the center of the room, with a small cave-like nook tucked off to the right. Two archways on the left led into the main room. VIP hugged the far-right wall beside the DJ booth. The office and restrooms ran along the left side, and a back bar and exit anchored the rear.

It was a maze—but it was *our* maze.

And when I walked into Rehab on a Saturday night and saw the floor packed tight, lights cutting through the smoke, music vibrating through the walls, something shifted inside me. The ghosts I carried didn't haunt me there.

I felt at home.

The same wild energy that had once pulled me into Heaven and Miami had evolved. It wasn't about escape anymore. It was about creation—about taking everything I had lived through and shaping it into something electric, something beautiful, something that made other people feel alive.

* * *

One of the earliest nights I remember at Rehab, I was standing at the back bar when one of the regulars started giving me a hard time about being gay. What made it sting even more was that the bartender took the regular's side. Word traveled fast, and when Chris heard what happened, he shut it down immediately. He stepped in and made it very clear that we were more than a team—we were a family, and family took care of each other. From that night on, no one questioned where I stood in the club hierarchy.

During this same period, Faye and I managed to get our hands on a popcorn machine, which opened the door for theme nights. One week, we threw a *Grease* party and dressed up as the Pink Ladies and Greasers. Next, I recruited Lexi again, and together we put on a full *Mommie Dearest* performance. I dressed as Joan Crawford and performed to a Cosmic Cat special mix of "No

Wire Hangers," and the crowd absolutely ate it up.

Not long after that, Chris handed me a box of promotional materials for *Dude, Where's My Car?*—T-shirts, signage, and a videocassette with either the whole movie or selected clips. I can't remember which, but I do remember plastering the club with signs and hyping the film like my life depended on it.

A few weeks later, my sister came to visit the club. After a packed Saturday night, we headed back to my apartment to crash. The next morning, she realized she didn't have her car. She couldn't remember where she'd parked it, and as she retraced her steps, she suddenly remembered handing her keys to someone—either a valet or a random person on the street. Possibly a homeless man. She wasn't sure.

True to *Dude, Where's My Car?*, the mystery unraveled itself later that evening when Kim Son called, asking if we planned on picking up the car we'd left with the valet the night before.

We did.

* * *

During the final days of Club Some, the owners, DJs, and promoters created an alternative to Rich's, and I remember when Madam Pussycat and Mister Terrific moved their promotions to this new venue. It was a much larger nightclub compared to the smaller after-hours setup at Some.

One night, when Rehab was extremely slow, Chris said, "Hey, let's close up and go out." He called Neil, the owner of Hyperia, and arranged for all of us to be comped. I was nervous as we approached the door—especially when I recognized Herald, the bouncer from Some, standing there. But Chris waved us through without hesitation, and we ended up filling Hyperia that night.

On another occasion at Hyperia, I was there with Cosmic Cat (Adam) and his partner at the time. The music was intense, and the tabs were too. The place was packed—bodies moving, lights pulsing—and suddenly Adam leaned toward me and said he was going to be sick. Seconds later, he projectile vomited behind a couch where no one could see him. The music never stopped. Neither did the party.

Hyperia holds so many memories for me. It was a castle of a club—towering, wild, and unforgettable.

* * *

One of the most memorable parties I ever threw was a month-long Sunday night DJ competition. When we first planned it, I had no idea it would attract some of the best up-and-coming DJs in the scene. That first night, the front room was set up like a lounge, the lights were on, and I walked around taking down the entrants' names.

Two names stood out immediately: Sista Stroke and Noize—the clear front-runners. Noize, whom I had never met or even heard of before, introduced himself with absolute confidence. He told me he was the most popular rising DJ from Clear Lake and that he had the competition "in the bag."

It certainly looked that way at first. One by one, each DJ took their turn on the decks. After each set, I gauged performance by crowd response—simple clap-meter style. Most of the applause was mild at best. No one came close to matching the roar the crowd gave DJ Noize. Round after round, he dominated, with Sista Stroke not far behind.

And then everything changed.

A relatively unknown DJ stepped up for his first public performance: Maximillian—Max. The moment he touched the tables, the energy in the room shifted. He instinctively understood what the crowd wanted, track after track, and within minutes, he had them in the palm of his hand. Cheers erupted louder than anything we'd heard all night. Noize's confidence suddenly didn't seem so solid.

There was one more memorable entry after Max. One of the house DJs had brought his protégé, DJ Alibi, who carried in a crate of records. With him was Erin—one of our regular rave girls—debuting as DJ Lullaby. She held her own and earned real respect from the room, but in the end, she couldn't surpass Max's explosive debut.

When we did the final handwritten vote, the result wasn't even close. It was a landslide. Max had won the entire competition—and, in many ways, the night.

* * *

Then, one weekend, the past shimmered back into view.

Kitty Meow, my dear friend and drag royalty from South Beach, flew in to host a circuit party called Combustion. I had spotted her name on a poster while printing out extra fliers for Rehab at Copy.com, a local copy shop in Montrose. With the excitement of reliving some of my memorable experiences in South Beach, we arranged to meet at their hotel upon arrival. This was one of the only times after I had left South Beach that I was able to connect with the life I had once had there. Jason and I went and had a great visit with Kitty (Shawn), who showed me the outfits she had planned for the weekend events.

She had placed us on the VIP list for the opening party, and when we showed up, I remember looking around for her for a few minutes until we saw each other across the club—smoke swirling, lights flashing. It was like time had folded in on itself. The hugs, the laughter, the shared memories of Miami—it was as if no years had passed at all. The first night of the weekend events was at Numbers, one of Texas's oldest nightclubs. The promoters had chosen a jungle theme; leopard prints and jungle-style trees were scattered about. I can remember Kitty being less than thrilled by the setup, walking around mostly bored. Then she spotted the leopard-print tablecloths, pulled one off a table, and wrapped it around her waist.

"This is more useful this way," she said.

We were survivors of an era that had burned fast and bright, and somehow, we were still standing.

That night, the crowd roared, the music shook the walls, and I stood in the center of it all—the master of the moment.

Ghost wasn't a mask anymore.

He was the part of me that refused to die—the fearless, creative, unstoppable spark that still burned even after the lights went out.

We skipped the Saturday night event because we were working at Rehab; however, Jason and I, along with Lexi, loaded up in the Rehab mobile and headed to Prague, a newly opened, extremely popular nightclub built inside a shuttered bank on Main Street in downtown Houston. I had been inside this venue once before, during the underground rave named Candyland--the safety-deposit boxes still had the keys in them.

We made it in time to see Martha Wash belt out "It's Raining Men," one of my anthems from back in the day, but Kitty did not make it, and I did not get to send her off that night.

We have reconnected on Facebook over the years. Now with social media, I have joined a special group named "Queens of South Beach" that was created to honor Paloma and others we have lost over the years. Sadly, Chyna, a legend herself and my upstairs neighbor during my time at Washington and 14th, has also passed away while writing this book.

* * *

Rehab became more than a club. It became a mirror of my rebirth—the evolution of a kid who once danced under borrowed lights into a man who built the stage himself. I wasn't just chasing the music anymore. I was writing it.

That year, Houston saw the birth of a new generation of club kids—kids who'd never seen Heaven, never danced at Liquid, never heard Madonna sing live. But they felt the same spark.

And when they saw me—the platforms, the makeup, the grin—they saw not a relic, but a survivor.

One night, a young promoter asked, "How do you do it? How do you keep going?"

I thought for a second and said, "Because even ghosts need to dance."

Ghost was back. Not the reckless boy who'd once burned through cities, but the man who'd risen from his own ashes—healed, focused, and in control of the music that once controlled him.

The lights of Rehab shimmered like true redemption.

And this time, I wasn't chasing the night.

I was conducting it.

16

Heaven Again

By 2001, I was at the top of my game.

Every night felt like a new opening, every weekend a fresh debut.

The city was mine—from the Montrose lounges to the massive warehouse raves that stretched until sunrise. My name carried weight again. If Ghost was on the flier, people showed up. DJs wanted my crowds, promoters wanted my touch, and I had the love of my life by my side. For the first time, the chaos didn't feel dangerous—it felt like destiny.

But before I reached that peak, something happened. In 1998, while I was still living in South Beach, Heaven—the club where it all began in Houston—burned down.

I remember hearing about the fire as if it were a dream. The news spread fast through Houston's nightlife circles—Heaven, the original sanctuary, gone in smoke. It felt symbolic, almost cruel.

By 2000, when I was fully back in Houston's nightlife scene, the old Heaven had been rebuilt and rebranded as South Beach.

South Beach—the name of the place that had shaped me, seduced me, nearly destroyed me—now stood as the phoenix rising from the ashes of my first home.

I never promoted there. I never ran a night under its neon roof. Not because I didn't want to or even try, having dropped off my cards and reached out to the person who ran the club for years (who must not be named), but the essence of the club kid culture was tarnished as a result of the scandal in New York, and I was not engaged to promote the new club. But I visited often—curious, nostalgic, and proud. The club pulsed with a new kind of beauty—sleek, luminous, modern—and the ghosts of our past seemed to shimmer just beneath the strobes.

The air smelled the same—sweat, smoke, perfume, and possibility. But I wasn't the same.

The kid from Heaven was gone.

The man from South Beach had lived and learned.

And the Ghost who stood there now knew that every paradise eventually burns.

* * *

During one of our weekend ventures, club-hopping in midtown, we happened upon DJ Fusion (David Piccone), one of my DJ idols from growing up, the voice I'd heard on the radio for years, and one of the people responsible for FUEL Fridays at Rich's, the very place where Ghost first appeared.

DJ Fusion was a Houston legend. His wife, Elizabeth—graceful, positive, and full of light—ran Social Butterfly Productions. Together, they were hosting events at Valentino's, a Louisiana-style mansion on Fannin Drive not far from uptown.

I attended their events regularly, became close with them, and tried to help promote their events. It was during this time that I began working at Atomic Music.

The song of this era was "It Feels So Good" by Sonique, whom I'd always loved back in South Beach when "I Put a Spell on You" was popular. I spent countless nights promoting, hoping this event would take off.

But then DJ Mark D swooped in and made a deal to reinvent the club as "Level," effectively ending our run.

This would come back to haunt me—literally—when I returned to the club later on.

By day, I worked as the marketing manager at Atomic Music in Montrose—a hub for DJs, dancers, and dreamers. Saturday mornings had their own rhythm. I'd arrive early to open the shop, and DJs would filter in throughout the day to sample new vinyl releases on the turntables, hunting for the perfect track to drop that weekend.

One Saturday, while opening the incoming mail, I pulled out a store copy of Boy George's *Essential Mix.* I slipped it onto the turntable immediately. The mix was a grand display of his eternal talent—layered, nostalgic, perfect. For two hours, that mix played on repeat while customers browsed, DJs sampled, and the Montrose morning sunlight cut through the store windows.

It felt like a transmission from the club kid elders—a reminder that the legends were still out there, still creating, still relevant.

I was restocking the house section when Ultra Naté's new album arrived. I'd been a devoted fan since "Free" became a South Beach anthem—one of those songs that defined an era, that made you believe in possibility even as everything around you was falling apart.

I slipped the CD into the player and started skipping through tracks.: dance remixes, club bangers, the usual progression. Then I hit track thirteen.

The title stopped me cold: "Ghost."

I stood there in the middle of Atomic Music, surrounded by vinyl and turntables and Saturday morning light, and felt the universe tilt slightly on its axis.

It wasn't about me—I knew that. Ultra Naté didn't know Mark Stevens from Houston. She'd never met the kid who painted spirals on his face or the man who'd rebuilt himself from ash.

But the synchronicity felt cosmic anyway.

I hit play.

The track was deep, introspective, haunting in the way only house music can be. It spoke about presence and absence. About moving through spaces unseen. About the part of yourself that lingers in a room even after you've left.

About being there and not there at the same time.

I thought about Heaven, about South Beach, about every club that had held my name in lights and every club that had forgotten it. I thought about the spiral—how it kept appearing, in logos and songs and moments like this.

I played the track three times in a row.

By the third listen, I understood:

The music had always known who I was.

Even before I did.

* * *

Eventually, I set up my own company: Ghostly Productions. I started small. I moved back to Montrose from the southwest side of town. I moved into an office apartment suite above the newly opened leather store on Westheimer Street.

A few connections here, a few favors there.

Within months, I was back in motion—hosting, curating, booking DJs, and designing nights that people would remember long after the lights came up. By day, I worked at Atomic Music. By night, I ran Ghostly Productions. The mission was simple: to craft nights that weren't just events, but experiences.

I booked local DJs like NutZ, Cosmic Cat, and Alibi, each spinning sounds that resurrected the spirit of the '90s while pushing it into something new—faster, deeper, rawer. Within a few months, people started calling me again—promoters, club owners, and friends who'd once watched Ghost fade away.

Now, they wanted him back.

The same name that had been whispered under strobe lights was glowing again—but this time, it stood for creation, not chaos.

Even though I wasn't officially a host or promoter at Rich's during this time, the crew did make our rounds there on occasion.

As I began prompting and getting to know groups of club goers, I met and became friends with Chad. He was roommates with a DJ of sorts who was great at mixing anything. There was a wannabe named Basil who always followed my crew around and asked too many questions. Lexi flat-out told them to get away from us and leave us alone.

And then there was the youngster, a twink of sorts who had hooked up with quite a few guys here and there during this time, and who had called and left a hysterical voicemail on Chad's voicemail (an old-school one that actually had a micro-cassette in it). Somehow, Lexi and Chad got together and had Chad's roommate mix a techno track with the part of the voicemail recording where the twink loudly says "I'm Not A WHORE!" We had it playing through the car's speakers just outside Rich's, with fliers stating the same thing plastered on all the windshields outside the club.

* * *

While it may be common nowadays that someone might identify with the area they are from, such as north, south, east, or west, back in the early 2000s, when I was promoting for Rehab, the Houston rap scene was bursting at the seams.

Mind you, I was at heart a techno/house-loving raver, circuit-boy club kid. At the time, I did not understand or appreciate what hip hop and rap were becoming, even though I heard the songs in the main room nightly, especially "Hot in Herre' by Nelly, and "In da Club" by 50 Cent.

I had developed a following of crews around the city: Lacy and the middle-class suburb crew from the northwest side, and Zoe Dalisa and the south-side Clear Lake crew were the two who most reliably attended our parties.

I had known Zoe from the south side since way back in my first days at the club. I did not realize it at the time, but Zoe would wind up feeding me to the wolves in the near future.

* * *

One of the most legendary venues of that time was The Eyeball Room—an abandoned Kmart in southwest Houston, turned into a cathedral of light and sound.

It wasn't just another party space. It was sacred ground.

It was the very same place where, back in 1993, I had wandered into one of my earliest raves—a wide-eyed kid in thrift clothes, chasing the unknown.

Now, I stood on that same concrete floor, not as a guest but as the creator—the one running the lights, the music, the madness. The same space that had once introduced me to the power of the night was now pulsing to my own rhythm.

When I walked through those doors on opening night, carrying my equipment and my fliers and my hopes, something shifted in my chest.

As the crowd filled in—ravers, club kids, baby gays holding hands nervously, veterans who remembered when this space was new—I felt something rare and perfect.

Not pride, exactly. Not nostalgia either.

Completion.

The universe had folded back on itself. Every trial, every club, every sleepless night, every moment of chaos and beauty had led me here—to The Eyeball Room, to this perfect loop of creation.

The music pounded. The lights melted into color. And I watched a thousand faces do precisely what I'd done eight years earlier:

Lose themselves.

Find themselves.

Become something new.

That night, I felt untouchable.

* * *

I made friends with Charles Solomon during Kitty's visit to Houston. They had taken a significant loss on that event and were seeking to recoup some of the funds. Charles Solomon and his investors had created a new group called the Spoiled Boys.

The Spoiled Boys was a card-carrying VIP group that met once a month for after-hours events at various Houston clubs. As a circuit-boys event, it drew large gatherings from across the area. I would dress in full costume and work the door with Charles.

We held these events at several clubs, including one I was promoting at The Pavilion—located next to the old Saks Fifth Avenue and run by John Findley, the publisher of *Concierge Magazine*, who had taken over the venue from the prior owners.

We held a packed Spoiled Boys event there one night. I have a picture somewhere of me as Pimp Ghost. Dressing up and working the ropes in my hometown to a sold-out party——it was one of the most memorable events I'd been part of. The venue was small, which made it feel even more packed. I remember the wallpaper literally peeling off the walls from all the sweat.

It was here that I created several nights, including Feel Fridays in collaboration with the Atomic Music crew. I remember there must have been some omen or curse on me because, on opening night, I went to the DJ booth to turn on the sound and accidentally pushed the wrong button, wiping out the $7,500 lighting program installed earlier that day.

This party premiered on March 16, 2001, around the time of my birthday. I had always considered my birthday lucky because I was born with a three-leaf clover-shaped birthmark on my upper arm. I remember the joke I was told from a young age: if I had waited a few more days to be born, maybe I would have wound up with the luckier four-leaf clover.

That didn't happen.

And this was the beginning of the end.

* * *

Continuing the Spoiled Boys' after-hours trend, I was introduced to the

Kaplan brothers, who were nightclub promoters and real-estate investors in Houston. The Kaplan Brothers owned Grasshopper and Europa. Europa, located on the southwest side of the Richmond strip, was one of my favorite clubs in Houston.

The warehouse was designed with five different rooms: an entrance room, a geisha lounge, the main dance floor with the Super Friends painted on the walls, a patio that wrapped around to a library straight out of Bruce Wayne's mansion, and pathways that led back through the geisha lounge.

The design was superb—each room flowing seamlessly into the next. At one point in the night, Charles Solomon came by, found me at the door, and asked me to get my friend out of the geisha lounge, where Zoe had created her own non-sanctioned VIP area and was saying only cute gays could enter.

Next, at the Grasshopper Lounge downtown, we did the BDSM theme. I dressed as Submissive Ghost with a mask. That night, one of the original club kids, Travis Boy, showed up at the door and attempted to pull me aside to get past the line; however, my role that night as submissive did not allow me to talk, so I had to wait to let him in, eventually taking a break and catching up with him to give him some drink tickets. I was supposed to host a ghost-themed Halloween party here under my banner, Ghostly Productions, but it was a dark time, and I dropped the ball several times and was unable to follow through with the production.

* * *

I had made friends with an original promoter from the club scene I had never met before. His name was Dhavid Ra. He was a well-known promoter and club kid from earlier days. Cosmic Cat had introduced us, and his style definitely inspired me. We were all hanging out one weekend, and I had acquired a vial of K, so I set up in the kitchen and began double-boiling it. At some point, I walked away to use the restroom. I left the K boiling, not realizing it was evaporating into the air vent, and I had inadvertently sent the entire house into a K-hole.

I can still remember coming to and hearing Cosmic Cat yelling, "Ghooost, what are you doing?" It sounded miles away, but it was merely Cosmic Cat and Dhavid Ra coming to and understanding what I had done.

And then there was the Dr Pepper can. I bought a mini-safe in the form of a Dr Pepper can. As you can imagine, I kept track of it since it held most of my money and party supplies. I would open a twelve-pack, place the can inside, and reseal the pack. Several weeks after I had it, I went to pick it up, and it was gone. Dhavid was cleaning my house and helping me design fliers around this time, and he couldn't find it either. Lo and behold, a few weeks later, once again at Rich's, when I came to my car, I found a "Ransom" letter with a picture of the Dr Pepper can on it. Lexi strikes again. The word shenanigans, which I first heard from Dhavid Ra, was part of the reason for the name of my next party: Vicious.

* * *

Mark D, the DJ from 104 KRBE Radio, who had taken over Valentino's and rebranded it as Level, agreed to let us host Thursday nights. DJ Alibi, DJ Cosmic Cat, and I signed on to do "Vicious" Thursdays.

The venue had new carpet, new bars, and upgraded lighting and sound. It looked flawless.

As opening night approached, I started getting calls from other promoters and DJs saying there was a problem. When I finally arrived—late, as usual—there was a vast crowd outside ready to party.

But the gates were locked.

Without any warning, the facility had been seized by the IRS earlier that day.

The party never happened. It never even started.

True to the name, the aftermath was vicious. As I was getting out of my car, I heard Cosmic Cat shouting, "Ghooooost, what the fuck!"—as if I had any idea the day would end this way.

I would see Mark D several times over the years. He avoided me like the plague after that night.

* * *

East downtown, in the area known as EADO, there was a space a few blocks from where the Houston Dynamo built their new stadium that had been a multiplex of strip clubs back in the 1970s, all connected and laid out. I made my way to EADO for the premiere of Privilege, opened by promoter extraordinaire Bobby Stark. DJ Fusion was one of the opening DJs here, and I went to support him. Although this venue did not last for long, a few months later, I would get a call from Chris Alan that he and Tony Montana—the guy who had famously promoted Karma Fridays south of Houston, where my good friend Summer S was a lead promoter—were taking over the venue and would be rebranding it under the name SPACE. I also attended, tried to get the word out about Chris, and helped promote and bring a crowd there. One of the opening parties was a foam party, and I dressed up in a complete surfing outfit with flippers, goggles, and all, and the parties were hopping for a few weeks there.

But at the height of it all, when the love was strong, the music was loud, and the city's pulse matched my own, something began to shift. The energy felt ... off.

The laughter still echoed, the crowds still danced, but there was a sharpness in the air—a tension I couldn't name.

Looking back, I can see it clearly: the glow that had carried me so far was turning into a spotlight I couldn't escape.

Rehab was thriving. Atomic was buzzing. I was working as a promoter at nightclubs, hosting the door for circuit parties and working the desk at Atomic Music, my name on every flier. But somewhere beneath the lights, something darker was building—whispers, warnings, strange faces in familiar places. I ignored it.

The night was too beautiful to imagine it ending.

* * *

I had befriended DJ Mikie Pratt and considered him a legend in the Houston Nightlife.

It was, of course, he, Sebastian (now known simply as Paris London) and I who had put Rehab on the map.

Mikie was unable to maintain a professional level of spinning at the club on a regular basis. Even though he helped bring in the record-breaking crowd one night, he was not allowed back into Rehab due to a few incidents of sloppiness on the decks; however, I remained friendly with him, hoping to help him be as successful a DJ as he had once been when I met him years earlier at STEAM. But this would take an extremely dark turn at the newly resurrected Westheimer street festival, which was no longer actually on Westheimer Avenue, but had been relocated to Allen Parkway along Buffalo Bayou.

I remember Ben, Mikie, and me hanging out that day, and at one point, we couldn't find Mikie for a while. When we did run back into him, he was coming out of the Bayou, retrieving something that had been almost knee-high in the dirty water. We left the street festival and went to hang out at one of the warehouses, Number Four's, across from Hyperia, and I can remember Mikey complaining of a severe itch on his leg. I encouraged him to clean up before we left that day. A few days later, I ran into some of Mikie's friends outside a club.

"Did you hear about Mikie?" one of them asked.

I hadn't.

The dirty bayou water he'd waded through was full of flesh-eating bacteria. By the time he went to the hospital complaining about the itch on his leg, the infection had spread too far. They'd had to amputate to save his life.

When I saw Mikie next, we went looking for prosthetics. He tried on several, testing balance and fit, his attitude somehow still upbeat despite everything.

"This one works," he said, taking a few careful steps.

He smiled, but I could see the weight of the loss in his eyes. The scene had taken so much from so many of us.

Houston's nightlife was evolving, sleek and glittering again, but quieter too—older somehow, more careful. The world was shifting. The innocence of the '90s was gone, replaced by something edgier, more fragile. And yet, as I stood beneath the lights of the new South Beach, watching the crowd undulate in time with the music, I couldn't help but smile.

Heaven had become South Beach.

The circle had closed.

The same spirit that once set me free had been reborn—in a new body, a new name, a new time.

And as the music swelled, I felt something rare and perfect:

Peace.

For the first time, I didn't need to be seen.

I just needed to remember.

17

The Calm Before the Storm

There's always a moment—just before the lights shift and the bass drops—when time seems to hold its breath.

That's what 2001 felt like.

A pause.

A shimmer before the crash. Everything looked perfect on the surface.

Houston's nightlife was alive again—reinvented, reborn, unstoppable.

We were older, wiser, and maybe a little more polished, but the pulse was still there, beating strong in Montrose, midtown, and every backroom that smelled of smoke and sweat. For the first time in a long time, I felt peace.

Not the quiet kind that comes from stillness, but the kind that comes from balance.

I had rebuilt my life from the ashes—Ghost was no longer a mask; he was a choice.

I had work, love, reputation, rhythm—the elements of a life I could finally call my own. On Sunday mornings, I'd drive through the empty streets, the skyline scintillating under early light.

Sometimes I'd stop by Atomic Music to stand in the silence before the doors opened, to hear the echo of everything I'd built faintly through the walls. People still called, still asked for appearances, still wanted Ghost to host, perform, create.

And I did—but with more control, more intention.

The nights were smaller now, but they meant more. There were moments, of course, when the past flickered through—whispers from Miami, faces I hadn't seen in years, the ghosts of clubs that no longer existed.

But they didn't haunt me anymore.

They reminded me. The nights of chaos had given way to rhythm.

The glitter had settled into gold. Still, in the back of my mind—and somewhere in my bones—I could feel it:

That faint vibration that comes right before everything changes.

Like static before a storm.

Like the last heartbeat before the break, the music never warns you when it's about to stop.

It just does. And when it did—when the lights flashed blue instead of white—I realized that calm had only been an illusion.

18

Ghost Writer

The night it all came crashing down started like any other. Saturday, March 17, 2001. St. Patrick's Day.

The rave was being thrown by Vinyl, a new record store trying to make its mark. I'd been invited to help promote the event and had sent Zoe to run the Atomic Music booth for me. The warehouse was buzzing—that familiar electricity that fills the air before the lights drop and the bass takes over.

It felt right. It felt like home. But behind the strobes and smiles, something darker was moving.

This event wasn't a party. It was a setup. And I should have known better, and I should have seen the signs, and I should have stayed home with Jason.

When the call came through, Jason pleaded with me to stay home. At this point, we had moved into an apartment above Steven Lawrence and Kay Kay, and I was on top of my game. Jason was working at Hastings Music, and I had parties running almost every night. I should have stayed home. We lasted six months.

Not because we didn't love each other—we did. But because Ghost came back louder than either of us expected, and Ghost consumed everything.

At first, Jason understood. He'd show up at Sanctuary, help me set up, stand by the door collecting covers while I worked the room. He'd watch me transform—white face paint, platforms, the spiral, lightning bolt—and smile like he was proud of what I was building.

But as the weeks went on, the parties became more frequent. Not just Saturdays at Sanctuary. Thursday nights at a midtown lounge. Friday pop-ups at underground spots. Sunday after-hours that bled into Monday mornings.

The late nights became every night. The parties became obsessions.

I'd leave the apartment at 10 p.m., promising to be home by 3:00. I'd stumble in at 7:00, smelling like smoke and sweat and someone else's perfume, to find Jason asleep on the couch—still wearing the clothes he'd put on to wait up for me.

I'd kiss his forehead. Whisper apologies—promise to do better.

And then Saturday would come, and I'd do it all again.

What I didn't know was that the Houston Police Department had been running an undercover sting. They were offering deals to anyone caught with party favors —

"Snitch on three, and you walk."

It was desperation disguised as justice. And that night, I walked straight into their trap.

When I arrived to check on the booth, a uniformed officer appeared out of nowhere.

He didn't ask questions.

He didn't shout.

He just said my name—my real name—and took my arm.

I remember the faces around me—wide-eyed, frozen. The lights flashing off badges instead of disco balls. The crowd's confusion turned to whispers. It was the sound of a record scratching the life out of a song.

I was escorted out through the main doors, the music still pounding behind me, as if the night refused to acknowledge what was happening.

For everyone else, the party went on.

For me, it was over.

* * *

I had been detained in handcuffs and sat in the back of a squad car with Zoe and a stranger who was asking me a lot of unusual questions.

Questions about my suppliers, my connections, and how the underground network operated. At that point, we were driven behind the building where massive tents and a processing center had been set up, with hundreds of detectives and personnel processing those the Houston Police Department had entrapped. They booked me, charged me, and held me. By the time I went to court, I had served thirty days in jail.

Long enough to feel the walls close in.

Long enough to understand how fast the music can stop.

When I finally got out, the hits came fast.

Jason told me he was leaving.

Atomic Music let me go.

I had let them down the most, as when I was arrested, people stole and carried away the setup. To this day, I regret this the most. I had let down those who had been the best to me.

And the name *Ghost*—once printed bold on fliers across Houston—was suddenly radioactive.

I tried to hold on.

My good friend, downstairs neighbor and world-renowned house DJ for the party I was throwing at the Citrus Room at the time, Steven Lawrence, picked me up from jail, and gave me a ride back to The Eyeball Room, where after thirty days surprisingly, my red Ford was still sitting in the parking lot untouched where I had left it a month earlier.

A few days later, I had dinner with John Findley, and he was flabbergasted at what I had been through, even mentioning that they had contributed to collecting funds to get me out, which had been disbursed somewhere but never put to the use they were meant for. As you read earlier, the day before I was arrested, I had started a party, Feel Fridays, which had gone well, other than the wiped lighting board. This ended the night I was arrested, as I was not around to keep it going, and my affiliation with Atomic ended.

* * *

When I was released from jail, I came home to find the apartment quiet. Too quiet.

Jason's sketchbooks were gone from the kitchen table. His toothbrush was missing from the bathroom. The Captain Janeway cutout Faye had given us was still on the wall, but everything else that made the space ours had disappeared.

On the kitchen table, a note in his handwriting:

I can't compete with the night. I'm not asking you to choose—I know you already have. I need to stop pretending I didn't lose.

You're going to do amazing things, Mark. I believe that. But I can't watch you disappear into Ghost again. It hurts too much.

I love you. That's why I'm leaving.

J

I stood there holding the note, still wearing my platforms, face paint smeared from hours of dancing, the sun pouring through the windows like an accusation. I should have run after him. Should have called. Should have chosen him over the night, over Ghost, over the endless hunger that never seemed to fill.

But I didn't.

I folded the note carefully. Put it in a drawer. Took off my platforms. Washed my face. And went to bed.

Because deep down, I knew he was right. Ghost had won. And Mark—the version of me that Jason had loved, the version that could exist in daylight without a mask—was already disappearing.

Years later, I'd understand what I'd lost. I'd realize that Jason had been the one person who saw me completely and loved me anyway. That the safety I felt with him was the thing I'd been searching for my entire life. But at the time, all I felt was the hollow where he'd been.

And by Saturday, the bass was already calling me back to fill it.

My relationship with Jason was the only time in my life I'd been in a genuine relationship.

And it was but a beat.

A beautiful, fragile, impossible beat.

Gone before I'd learned to hold onto it.

* * *

I kept promoting small events with John Findley and Charles Solomon, clinging to the last remnants of the scene I'd built. But the crowds felt smaller now, the lights dimmer, the energy fractured. The innocence was gone—replaced by suspicion, by silence.

Even the music sounded different.

And then came 9/11.

The world stopped.

So did we.

At least for the time being.

* * *

I didn't leave Houston all at once.

I leaked out of the city like air escaping a balloon.

By 2001, after 9/11 left the entire world stunned and holding its breath, the nightlife I once shaped felt like a foreign country. The last few attempts to revive myself as a promoter came out thin and shaky, like echoes of a voice I once had. The scene had shifted, and I was drifting through it like a stranger wearing an old costume that no longer fit.

Ben appeared during this time—a soft landing in a challenging year—and for a while, we stayed with one of my sister's friends in the Memorial area. It was a quiet, manicured neighborhood, the kind where sprinklers clicked on at dawn, and everything smelled like cut grass and forgotten wealth. My life, by contrast, smelled like bleach, cigarette breath, and exhaustion.

Then I moved into an apartment near Alabama Street.

Then I moved again.

And again.

A ghost doesn't settle—he floats.

I eventually made my way to Bay City, hiding out with my brother and his family. I tried a new venture there—another restaurant, another dream in a long line of dreams I tried to force into existence. For three weeks, it felt possible. For three weeks, the walls buzzed with ambition. Then it collapsed like a sandcastle under a wave.

So I packed myself up—again—and floated to Katy. And where does a drifting man always end up?

Denny's.

Always Denny's.

I was back in a manager's uniform, counting drawers, wiping down counters, the heavy scent of fryer oil clinging to my clothes like regret.

I wasn't searching for purpose.

I was trying to move without falling apart.

* * *

Eventually, the tide pulled me to Baytown, where I slipped into small-time promoting—the minor league of nightlife. I hosted a wet T-shirt contest at a local bar, the kind of event that feels sticky even in memory. But it was there, amid spilled beer and neon signs buzzing like dying flies, that I heard the rumor:

Rehab was back.

Under the new name and logo of Pink Monkey.

And not only that—Chris and his crew hadn't just revived it. They had taken over Rich's, too—the place where my legend first caught fire.

It didn't feel real.

It felt like being haunted by my own past.

I tried to re-enter Houston nightlife the way someone might try to enter a house they once owned—quietly, reverently, hoping the walls remembered them.

But Houston had changed its locks.

My promoter rival, Jermaine Flowers, was thriving—running nights at Pink Monkey and Rich's with the kind of youthful momentum I no longer had access to. He worked in the mall, surrounded daily by the exact demographic nightlife feeds on:

Young. Restless. Paid. Hungry.

My crowd?

Denny's regulars. Truck drivers, retirees, hungover line cooks, and teenagers drinking coffee they didn't pay for. Not precisely the army of nightlife disciples needed to resurrect Ghost.

Still, I tried.

I grabbed fliers, rearranged my hair, and forced the old swagger into my step. Chris Alan even threw down a challenge—a spark from the past:

"Show me if you still got it—Pied Piper style."

My heart leapt at that.

Ghost twitched under my skin.

But when I stood in front of Rich's that night, holding those fliers like old prayer cards, the truth washed over me in a hot wave:

No one was following.

The Pied Piper had lost his tune.

I was standing in the same spot I once ruled, but the air no longer recognized me.

It was like visiting your childhood home and finding strangers living in it.

* * *

Not long after, I left Denny's—again—and drifted into a series of small jobs. One of them brought me into the orbit of Lisa, a tough, sharp-witted lesbian with a protective streak as wide as the Gulf of Mexico. Lisa's mother, Connie, had the kind of big 1980s hair that defied physics and demanded respect. Their energy was the kind that could lift a dead night into a party.

They helped me land a job as an activities director at an old folks' home.

For a few months, I lived in a world of bingo cards, hallway races with wheelchairs, and residents who moved slowly but spoke loudly. I made them laugh. They made me feel human.

But even with Lisa and her crew backing me, even with their loud joy and bright energy at my side, I couldn't bring a crowd back to Rich's.

We walked in together, trying to reclaim something that no longer existed. The club swallowed us whole—not angrily, not cruelly—just indifferently.

That was almost worse.

Trouble found me again soon after. By then, it didn't even have to try. I was unraveling, thread by thread, drifting without Ghost's glow to hold me together.

This time, the Judge didn't send me to a detox or a halfway house.

This time, the Judge sent me to real rehab—a county-run therapeutic community. Six months.

Six months without clubs.

Six months without mixers, promoters, and DJs.

Six months without Ghost.

The first night I lay in that narrow cot listening to other men snoring, coughing, crying—some pacing, some praying—it hit me:

I wasn't coming back to nightlife.

Not the way I once was.

Rehab for real wasn't a pause.

Rehab was a burial.

* * *

In the distorted words of Pianoheadz, which echoed through my mind like a eulogy, "It's over for me."

And it was.

That day didn't just mark the end of a chapter—it marked the end of a cultural species. A generation born from glitter and warehouse walls. The last breath of the original club kids. The fading out of an era when nightlife wasn't just entertainment—it was identity, Sanctuary, performance art, and rebellion.

The glowsticks went dark.

The platform boots stopped stomping.

The club kids, once immortal in their glitter armor, scattered like confetti caught in a gutter drain.

The DJs rose as new gods.

The scene rearranged itself.

And Ghost—once a name spoken with curiosity, admiration, envy—faded quietly into the shadow he had always pretended to be.

I did not die.

But I did disappear.

The world changed.

And I changed with it.

And for the first time in my life—without the makeup, the music, the crowds, the chase—I had no idea who I was supposed to rise as next.

Guess Who?

Thirty years later, I'm writing this from a desk in rural Texas.

Not a club. Not a stage. Not under strobes or neon or the thump of bass that once felt like a second heartbeat.

Just a desk. A laptop. Silence.

Outside my window, the landscape stretches flat and endless—nothing like the skylines of Houston, Miami, or New York that once framed my nights. The only lights out here are stars and the occasional headlight cutting through the darkness on a county road.

I'm fifty now. Sober. Taking care of myself and my family.

And for the first time in decades, I'm trying to make sense of who Ghost was—and who Mark is.

I had imagined writing this book for years.

The memories would hit at random—standing in a grocery store and suddenly hearing a song from Liquid, or catching my reflection in a window and remembering the spiral I used to paint on my face.

Flashbacks weren't always painful. Sometimes they were beautiful.

In the years between relapses, I even tried to return to the scene—not as Ghost, but as something new.

In 2024, my stepfather—the man who'd helped me avoid doing hard jail time when I returned from Miami in 1998—fell ill. I moved back home to care for him. When he passed, I stayed with my mother. For the first time in decades, I had time—real time—to sit still and remember. I was working from home in a customer-service role at a law firm, and things had slowed down considerably to the point where I had half my time each day with nothing to do. I sat down to write this book in 2025 after being laid off from my job, having my home office set up, and having plenty of time on my hands to write.

For years, I told myself I'd write it "someday." But someday became twenty years, and in those twenty years, I buried friends, lost careers, survived jail, earned degrees, and counseled others through the same addictions that nearly killed me.

I needed distance to see the story clearly.

I needed sobriety to tell it honestly.

And I needed to understand: Ghost wasn't a mistake. He was a lifeline for a kid who didn't know how to survive any other way.

After the dust settled from my final arrest, I did what I always did: I rebuilt.

Treatment in Harris County. Meetings. Accountability. The slow, unglamorous work of getting sober.

I wish I could say my addiction ended there.

It didn't.

But something shifted. I went back to school—something I'd started and abandoned an indecent number of times. This time, I finished. Bachelor's degree. Then a Master's. I began chasing credentials the way I'd once chased lights.

I became a college counselor. Adjunct professor. Then, a chemical-dependency counselor: the kid who'd spent a decade high was now the one telling others how to get clean.

I was good at it, too.

I understood the language of escape in ways my colleagues with their textbook knowledge never could. I knew what it felt like to need something so badly you'd trade everything—your name, your future, your freedom—to feel okay for a few hours.

I got published and presented at conferences. Built a career I was proud of.

And then I relapsed.

Lost everything.

Rebuilt again.

And relapsed again.

The pattern repeated itself twice more over the next decade—success, relapse, destruction, recovery. Each time I thought, *This time is different.* Each time, I was wrong.

I spent six months in Brazoria County on drug possession charges. Then more treatment. Then rebuilding. Again.

Two years of my life—total—spent incarcerated for minor possession.

Two years for carrying what I used to consume in a single weekend without consequence.

The system doesn't care about context. It doesn't care that you once had degrees or a career or that you counseled others through the same thing. It just cares about the charge.

Each time I got out, I'd swear I was done. Each time, Ghost would whisper from somewhere deep:

Remember when you were untouchable?

Remember when the night was yours?

But I wasn't that person anymore. And pretending I could be—even for a weekend—always ended the same way.

In the years between relapses, during the stretches of sobriety and success, I tried returning to the scene.

Not as Ghost—I knew better than that. But as someone adjacent. A producer. A host. A reminder of what used to be.

I opened a nightclub with Keoki—the superstar DJ whose sets had once defined a generation's sound. Working beside him felt surreal, like stepping into a memory I wasn't sure was mine.

I brought James St. James to Houston for an event. The man whose books I'd read, whose interviews I'd memorized, whose name was synonymous with the golden age of club culture. We stood backstage, and for a moment I was sixteen again, watching *The Jenny Jones Show*, imagining a world where I could be that free.

I hosted Lady Bunny and Bugie at parties that felt like resurrections—brief flashes of the old magic, the old fire.

Those nights were beautiful.

But they were also dangerous.

Because standing beside legends reminded me how close I'd come. How much I'd lost. How easy it would be to slip back into the person who thought the night could save him forever.

I couldn't stay in that world.

Not because I didn't love it.

But because loving it had nearly killed me.

Those stories—the later nights, the full-circle moments, the surreal experience of meeting your heroes and realizing you'd become one too—those are for another book.

This one is about the kid who became Ghost.

Not the man who tried to resurrect him.

In recovery, we talk about people, places, and things.

Change them to stay sober.

But when I look back at my story, people, places, and things were everything. I have made contact while writing this book with many of those whom you have read about. Thinking back on my days in the '90s, before cell phones were the norm, we had no way to connect other than the club. We did not have social networks online. The social network was real people you connected with and stayed in contact with, week to week.

Some of the people in this book are gone.

There are legends of South Beach who are no longer with us--too many to name, but those I knew I mention here, in this book, to honor their legacies.

HIV. Overdoses. Time. The casualties of a scene that burned too bright.

But some survived.

I see them on Facebook—older, grayer, quieter, some still throwing parties. Some are still mixing and performing. Some are raising kids, and even have grandkids now. Some like me, sitting at desks in places we never imagined, writing stories about nights that feel like visions from someone else's past.

We're the generation that built the rave.

We're also the generation that survived it.

If you're reading this and you see yourself in these pages—the kid who doesn't fit, the one chasing bass and lights and belonging—know this:

The night can save you.

But it can also swallow you whole.

Ghost taught me how to be fearless. But Mark taught me how to survive.

I don't regret the platforms, the spiral, the chaos. I don't regret Heaven or Miami or the nights that nearly killed me.

Because they also made me.

This book isn't a warning. It's not a cautionary tale.

It's proof that you can fall apart and rebuild yourself a hundred times.

That reinvention is always possible.

That even ghosts learn to rest.

I'm not chasing the night anymore.

But I'll never forget the way it felt to float through a room--as a Ghost.

19

Conclusion: Fade Out

When the towers fell, so did the world I had built, or at least it began to crumble. The music stopped, the parties ended, and the faces that once filled the night scattered into memory. Ghost became just that. A whisper. A story people told about a time when we believed the night could last forever.

But the truth is, nothing lasts forever. Not the lights, not the music, not even Ghost.

What remains are the stories—flashes of color, rhythm, and madness— proof that for one brief, blinding moment, we lived louder than anyone else dared to.

* * *

The world I lived in doesn't exist anymore—not in the way it once did.

The clubs are gone, the DJs have faded and transitioned to social media, and most of the people who made those nights unforgettable have moved on or vanished into time.

But sometimes, when I hear the faint thump of a baseline from a passing car or catch the glint of glitter under a streetlight, I'm right back there—under the strobes, surrounded by music, wearing the name Ghost like armor and invitation all at once.

People ask me sometimes if I miss it—the parties, the fame, the chaos.

The truth is, I miss the *feeling.*

That electric moment when the lights dropped, the DJ built the beat, and the entire room seemed to inhale at once—that heartbeat of unity, of being fully alive and seen.

In that moment, we weren't just dancing; we were creating something sacred.

Every night was a small rebellion against everything that told us we couldn't be free.

The club kid movement, in all its madness, was about more than shock or spectacle.

It was a form of resistance—a creative uprising.

We came from every background, every wound, every dream.

We dressed like superheroes and cartoons because we refused to be ordinary.

We lived out loud because the world outside the club doors tried to keep us quiet.

Our makeup was our manifesto. Our fashion was our armor. Our nights were our stories.

But even revolutions burn out. The lights fade, the records stop, and the faces blur into memory. And when the music finally stopped for me—after the arrests, the raids, the chaos, and the silence—I had to learn who I was without the costume, without the crowd, without Ghost.

That was the hardest part.

Because Ghost had been my freedom, my shield, my escape.

Losing him meant learning how to stand still in my own skin again.

Over the years, I've come to understand that Ghost never really died.

He evolved.

He lives in every creative risk I take, every story I tell, every room where I choose to show up as my most authentic self.

Ghost wasn't just a character—he was the part of me that refused to disappear. The part that still believes in the power of music, art, and community to change lives.

It is important to note that, while writing this memoir, the person considered the original club kid, Michael Alig, is no longer living.

I have chosen to focus on my own life and experiences over the years, but I must pay tribute to the founders—Michael, James, and, of course, Angel.

Their stories are laid out in detail in the book Disco Bloodbath and the film Party Monster, and their impact on youth culture and nightlife will never be forgotten.

In South Beach and New York, I had the honor and privilege of meeting and becoming friends with many legends who are no longer with us—including Paloma, Chyna, and Pagan. As mentioned earlier, Joval and Shawn Palacious, Kitty Meow, have created a Facebook page honoring the fallen heroes of this era.

They are all mentioned throughout these pages, and I hope I have done their trailblazing and significance justice.

They built the stages we danced on. They made the night feel limitless.

The club kid style was already fading when I took on the name and look of Ghost.

It is all but gone now, replaced by the drag scene in full force—which carries its own brilliance, beauty, and power.

Still, I hope these stories spark interest in the character-driven style and performance-art culture that once ruled the club scene—when creativity was the only ticket that mattered.

If even one new artist, dreamer, or misfit feels inspired to build something wild and original after reading this, then Ghost still serves his purpose.

I wrote this story not to glorify the past, but to honor it—to remember the people, the places, and the moments that shaped me and so many others.

For every friend we lost, every night we thought would never end, every time we danced because it was the only thing that made sense—this is for them.

If there's one truth I've carried with me, it's this:

Life, like nightlife, is a cycle of reinvention.

You burn, you fade, you rise again.

The trick is knowing when to let go and when to start over.

I don't know if I was really *the last club kid*—maybe just the last one from a specific time, a particular city, with a certain kind of magic.

But I do know this: for a moment, under the lights, we were infinite.

And if you were ever there—if you ever danced, laughed, loved, or *felt alive*—then you were part of it too.

Ghost lives on in the echoes, in the memories, in the stories we tell when the music's long since stopped.

And that, I think, is the real afterlife.

www.ingramcontent.com/pod-product-compliance
Lightning Source LLC
Chambersburg PA
CBHW071738150726
47998CB00005B/1709